The Exegesis Seminar

by

A K Webb

First Edition

ISBN: 978-1500597153 (Print)

Also available in e book

Also by A. K. Webb

Rough Diamond
Past Tense

You can find out more about the author at:
www.akwebb-author.co.uk

Acknowledgements

I would like to thank the people who helped me with this book. They are: Those Exegesis graduates who generously provided me with their subjective input, Judi Smith from Jastrad Publishing who read through endless drafts and helped me with the book's readability and Vicky Beale for giving the proof a thorough going over. Thanks also to Karen Cook and the other kind souls who acted as my non Exegesis reading guinea pigs.

And finally, thanks to Steve for providing the cover photo and cover artwork.

Exegesis

Dictionary meaning

Exegesis – explanation, interpretation

Pronounced - eksi jee sis

Seminar meaning

Exegesis – unravel, enlighten

Pronounced – eks edge eh sis

Knowing others is wisdom. Knowing yourself is enlightenment. Lao Tzu

Find out why you are the way you are. Why you feel the way you do. Why you get sad, happy, angry or frightened. Discover how you function and the truth will change your life.

In the nineteen eighties The Exegesis seminar was an enlightenment programme that was so powerful and had such a profound effect on people that it came to the attention of the British Establishment.

This is the first book written from the viewpoint of those who actually completed the seminar.

An unbiased re-enactment of the Exegesis seminar that provides a faithful account of the programme which changed lives forever.

Introduction

A lot has been written about Exegesis and its associated business Programmes Ltd. Much of the comment has been critical and based on a misunderstanding of the training programme and a misrepresentation of what Exegesis actually was. There were sensationalist claims of a brainwashing cult in which graduates were coerced to work for the organisation against their will. Newspapers carried lurid stories about people being forced to reveal their sexual fantasies and of being shouted at, harangued and bullied as part of the seminar process. Wild accusations such as these led to a question being raised in The House of Commons about its activities.

Unsurprisingly, the media focused on individuals, especially celebrities, who participated in the seminar. More recently there was renewed newspaper comment when it emerged that a close friend and adviser of Cherie Blair, the wife of the then Prime Minister, was an Exegesis graduate.

Throughout all of the reporting and comment on Exegesis virtually nothing has been written from the perspective of the participants, the ordinary people like me, who took the seminar.

My aim is to present The Exegesis seminar programme from the viewpoint of the people who undertook the training in the hope of gaining some sort of change or improvement in their lives. I have attempted, in this book, to provide a written re-enactment of the training and a feeling of what it was like to be a part of those extraordinary events.

So what was Exegesis?

The Exegesis seminar programme was formulated by Robert D'Aubigny in the late nineteen seventies. A great part of it was based on EST or Erhard Seminar Training. EST was, at one time, the most popular and well known enlightenment programme in the United States of America. (Latterly there were EST programmes in Britain, Europe and the rest of the world.) There were however, notable differences between the two programmes. Robert D'Aubigny took Werner Erhard's EST and remodelled it from the US orientated programme to a more UK friendly one. The structure of EST fitted the American psyche brilliantly and Exegesis resonated with the British in the same way.

In 1983, at the Mind and Body Exhibition, Robert D'Aubigny was asked what Exegesis was. He glibly remarked that it was a vehicle for recruiting telephone marketing personnel for Programmes Ltd. While this was in fact true it was always more than that. Only a small percentage of Exegesis graduates went on to work for Programmes Ltd. That was always a matter of individual choice. For the vast majority of people who completed the seminar, Exegesis was a dynamic course that profoundly changed their lives for the better.

The seminar itself, acted like a mental detox programme. It removed the barriers that prevent people from being how they would like to be. For those who completed the seminar, the benefits were tangible and lasting. The process of undertaking this form of therapy allowed them to flourish in ways that they would never have thought possible.

For those of you who have done the seminar, you may notice some discrepancies with the order of events. This is because the order often changed from seminar to seminar. These were slight adjustments that were dependent on the pace of the seminar. You may also notice that whilst some of the earlier seminars were three or four days in length the re-enactment is of the five day seminar. I did this simply to represent the seminar at its fullest. Consideration also needs to be given to the fact that the seminar is a very personal experience and what may seem pertinent to one person may be meaningless to another. One thing that I have discovered whilst discussing the programme with others is that no two persons' memory of the seminar or their experiences of it are ever the same. Whilst I have provided an honest account of my experience along with my observations of some of the comments and conduct of fellow trainees, my representation of the seminar and the concepts behind it is a personal one and this should also be borne in mind.

For those of you who have not been through the seminar, please keep going and finish the book. The seminar was a joyous and exhilarating experience but at times incredibly tedious and tiring. As part of the seminar process participants, or trainees as they were generally called, were encouraged to *share* whatever it was that they were experiencing or had experienced as well as any comments or questions that they may have had. The room in which the seminar took place was held as a safe environment for the trainees to say, literary, anything they liked. Exploring the trainees' various experiences was a massively important part of the seminar process and, needless to say, took up many hours. To make the book readable I have shortened these sessions and indicated this by adding a gap and a brief précis of the nature of the sharing taking place. I have, however, tried to recreate the experiences of tedium, tiredness, joy and elation as well as a feeling of what it was like to be in the room.

It was an oft mentioned phrase during the seminar, 'keep your foot in the room and you will *get it*'. In the case of this book the phrase should be, 'keep your eye on the page and you will *get it*'.

Getting it, or gaining enlightenment, was the promise of the seminar and for the vast majority of graduates it delivered on its promise.

You may ask, what qualifies me to write a truthful account of The Exegesis seminar? Firstly, I consider myself to be a reasonably normal, run of the mill sort of person. I have no leanings towards any religion and I am, and have always been, wary of cults. I pride myself on being cautious and clever enough not to be taken in by spurious claims of wonder treatments.

Additionally, although whilst researching this book I have recently met with a number of Exegesis graduates along with a few of the people who had worked for Programmes, I never have had and still do not have any lasting association with Exegesis, Programmes or any of the people who were closely involved with those organisations. I have purposely avoided any consultation with those persons and have focused on the views and information provided by individuals who participated in the seminar as trainees.

I believe that these facts allow me to provide a faithful re-enactment of what is essentially a subjective experience, in an objective manner.

Finally, I have participated in the Exegesis programme and the EST programme, from which Exegesis took many of its concepts and practices, on more than one occasion. This has allowed me to present a brief comparison between the two programmes at the end of this book.

In the re-enactment I have retained the names of Robert, Kim and Nick as they were important figures in both Exegesis and Programmes. Whilst the descriptions of the trainees are representative of the people who attended the seminar, all of the names and the sharing attributed to them do not relate to any real person. The trainers' names have also been plucked from my imagination.

Before the Seminar

The way in which I was introduced to Exegesis was, in hindsight, pretty much the same as almost everyone else that I spoke to: I was cajoled into it by someone who had just done the seminar, in my case a friend of mine. I agreed to participate because the friend in question was consistent in their enthusiasm for what they had *got* from it and I had noticed a positive change in their behaviour which fascinated me. They were more confident, they fairly fizzed with an energy and vigour that had not been present before and they appeared to possess a calmness and clarity that, once again, had not previously been evident. That, and as I mentioned before, they were persistent. My friend told me that the cost of the seminar was two hundred pounds and it would be the best couple of hundred quid I had ever spent. I agreed to attend a preview which was being held the following Wednesday evening at the Metropole Hotel on the Edgware Road in London.

When I arrived at the Metropole my friend told me that she would be attending the final Wednesday of her seminar and I should proceed on my own. She directed me into a conference room, where sat perhaps fifty other similarly introduced prospective Exegesis trainees, before disappearing off to where she had to go.

To me, the preview resembled a sales pitch where graduates of the training provided examples of how the seminar had improved their lives. Some of these graduates stated that the seminar had a massively positive effect on their careers, others focused on items such as an improvement in their relationships or an exponential increase in self confidence and energy levels. The familiar theme was that you could achieve any goal that you set for yourself if you completed the training.

Personally, I viewed all of these claims with a degree of scepticism. Additionally, I was amused when, on leaving the preview, those who said that they would not be attending the seminar or had yet to decide were forced to endure an interview with one of the graduates before they were allowed out of the room.

Whilst I had already made up my mind to participate, it is in my nature to behave doggedly or in a bloody minded fashion when presented with a situation like this. Consequently, I steadfastly refused to sign up that evening and regarded my refusal as a sort of triumph over the forceful and persuasive Exegesis graduates. Needless to say, the following day, I telephoned and signed up to attend the next available seminar.

I was told that the training takes place over five full days and three evenings and that there would be a logistics and preparation evening the following Wednesday at seven thirty at the Great Western Hotel by Paddington Station. The person on the telephone, an enthusiastic, young sounding man named Phillip, said that I should pay my friend the fee for the seminar, which she would pass on. The following day I paid my friend the two hundred pounds. She gave me a delegate questionnaire form to fill in and take with me.

Part 1

The Psychological Soap Opera

First Wednesday evening

I arrive at the hotel on this first Wednesday and make my way to the designated room, the room where the action is taking place. The doors are open and I wander in. Two people at the door check my name and give me a tag with my first name hand written on it. The room itself is large, possibly an old ballroom. It is ornate in the same style as the rest of the late Victorian station hotel. It has cream coloured architrave panelled walls and a lush red carpet with a swirling pattern. At the front of the room is a low stage that might have accommodated a band at some time but looked now, like it had been added as an afterthought. On the stage stands a lectern along with an easel with a white flip chart pad for writing on. Opposite each other, set up high on the side walls, are two large round modern clocks.

Seated inside the room are perhaps seventy or eighty nervous and expectant looking trainees. I sit down. The chairs have been set out in two blocks of eight across and eight deep. The way in which they are arranged allows for an aisle of some two and a half metres wide to run between the two blocks. There is also space to walk up and down in front of the low stage and at the sides of the blocks of chairs. On the right hand side are a further dozen or so chairs placed with their backs against the wall, facing out.

Gradually the seats fill. There must be more than one hundred and twenty people. Some arrive a few minutes late. One, a woman in her early thirties who is wearing a bright headscarf arrives twenty minutes late.

The proceedings appear to be directed by two trainers. One has a badge that says Nick and the other a badge that says Elizabeth. The evening is taken up with our questionnaires being looked at individually. Our personal information is checked, such as names, addresses and phone numbers as well as details of any prescription medication we may be taking and medical conditions we might have. I noticed that four or five people have forgotten their questionnaires. They are given new ones and sent to a table at the back of the room to complete them. It seems a bit like the first day at school. We are asked to reconfirm that we will abide by the rules of the seminar which Nick refers to as our 'agreements'. Among these agreements are the requirements that, for the two weeks in which the seminar will be held, we will not drink alcohol, nor will we take non-prescribed drugs, or use headache relief drugs such as paracetamol and aspirin. Smokers agree to not use any nicotine replacement aids whilst inside the training room. We also agree to be on time, to keep our name badges on whilst in the room, to not leave the room unless directed by a trainer and to not speak in the room unless directed to do so by a trainer. We agree to leave bags, watches, cigarettes, food and drink at the back of the room when we enter and not to bring any recording equipment into the room. It is not one of the agreements but Nick recommends that we wear comfortable clothes.

At nine thirty the trainer Elizabeth asks if anyone will have any difficulty getting to the seminar venue by nine o'clock on Friday morning. A few hands go up and Elizabeth, with amazing efficiency, organises the logistics of trains, buses and lifts with other trainees.

At ten thirty we are finished and sent home with a reminder to keep to our agreements and especially, to be on time on Friday.

'The seminar has started,' says Nick. 'It started when you entered the room this evening. Remember, you must keep to your agreements. The next session starts on Friday morning at nine a.m. sharp. Anyone arriving late will not be allowed to enter the room and will lose the two hundred pounds that they have paid.'

First Friday

I am anxious not to be late so I arrive in Paddington at eight fifteen and go to a cafe around the corner and wait. When I get to the hotel at eight fifty there are a few people that I recognise from the previous Wednesday evening standing outside smoking. Inside there are thirty or so people waiting outside the room. At a few minutes to nine the doors open and we enter. We are relieved of our coats, scarves, bags and watches and given badges with our names on. The trainers who undertake this procedure are noticeably stern looking, automated and unsmiling. One of them is the trainer Nick who appeared to be in charge on the Wednesday. I say hello to him and smile but he simply stares blankly at me. I am slightly unsettled by his expressionless demeanour. There are perhaps ten trainers, male and female, directing the incoming trainees. The men wear suits and shirts and ties. The women wear matching jackets and skirts with white blouses. In the room the same lectern and white flip chart stand on the stage. I notice that the two clocks on the side walls have been tapped over so we can't read the time. In a short while we are all seated and facing the stage. There is a buzz of noise, of conversation and pleasantries exchanged, as we wait. I am seated at the end of the third row from the front, by the centre aisle. The person sitting next to me is called Cath. She tells me that she was persuaded to do the seminar by her ex husband who, she says, has almost become a pleasant person after completing it.

Whilst I chat to Cath I watch as some of the trainers sit on the

17

chairs at the side of the room. I notice that the last trainer at the side has a large tape recorder and microphone placed by his chair. It seems that we will be taped. A further three or four trainers position themselves at the rear of the room.

The trainer called Nick walks purposefully to the front.

'The seminar has started and you have agreed not to speak whilst you are in the seminar room, unless directed to do so,' he says.

Nick's voice is unexpectedly loud, precise and clear. His statement and verbal delivery has the effect of quieting the buzz of conversation to first, a murmur and then silence. I notice that a few people already start to look anxious.

Nick then proceeds to count us.

A few minutes later the door at the rear opens and the lady with the bright headscarf who had been late on the Wednesday enters. I can see two more trainers stood outside holding the door open for her. As she comes in Nick, the trainer at the front, who is counting, strides to halfway down the aisle between the two rows of seated trainees. He stops her and states that as she is late she will not be allowed to participate. Two other trainers come forward and escort her out of the room despite her spluttered apologies, excuses and objections. This has the effect of raising the level of anxiety amongst some of the trainees to an even greater level. Throughout this interlude the trainers maintain the same expressionless demeanours.

After a few more minutes the door opens again and a woman, probably in her late twenties to early thirties enters and walks along the side of the two blocks of seats and on to the stage. She is nice looking with blond bobbed hair. She is wearing a blue business suit with a knee length skirt and a crisp white blouse.

'My name is Kim,' she says.

18

Her voice is sharp, clear and even louder than Nick's.

'I am here to ensure that you all *get it*. Whatever happens, if you stay in the room, you will *get it*.'

A few hands go up.

'I want you to listen to what I am saying for the moment. You will be able to ask questions and say what you like later.'

The hands go back down. The person sitting on the other side of the aisle to me, a guy named Jeff, shifts uncomfortably in his seat and mumbles something.

'In fact it is essential to the training that you participate actively,' she says. 'This is called sharing. You may share by asking a question or by answering a question. You may share by expressing a view, sharing an experience or sharing how you feel. You may share how you feel about anything. The way in which we share is this.'

Kim raises her arm.

'We raise our hand like this and wait to be picked. Then, when you have been picked, you stand up and speak. When we have finished you sit down. You must remain seated unless you are sharing. We acknowledge anyone who shares by doing this.'

Kim claps.

'This is clapping. Whatever that sharing may be, we acknowledge the input by clapping. Whether you agree with what's been said or not, you still acknowledge the person who has shared. If you disagree with them you may share your disagreement in the manner described. The only time that you may speak when you are not sharing is if you cannot hear what the person sharing is saying, in which case you may shout, "Can't hear." Any questions?'

A couple of hands go up. Kim picks a girl called Celia.

'Yes Celia.'

Celia is tall with long brown curly hair. I can't see her clearly because she is on the other side of the room, in the other block of chairs and behind where I am sitting.

'What if I need to go to the toilet?' she asks after she has stood up.

'You have agreed to stay in the room until you are told you can leave, you must make sure that you do whatever you need to do before you enter the room.'

'What if I can't wait,' she says.

'Then you'll just have to pee in your pants,' says Kim.

(Laughter)

'Thank you Celia.'

Celia sits down looking a little shocked and bewildered.

'Acknowledge Celia please,' says Kim. 'It isn't difficult to remember,' she adds.

There is a sarcastic note to her voice.

We clap.

'Yes Ray.'

'What time does this finish?' a male voice enquires.

Once again I can't see who asked the question. Ray's voice has come from behind where I am sitting.

'When it finishes,' Kim replies.

She reminds us again to acknowledge the person who has just asked the question.

(Applause)

'If it's late I'll have difficulty getting home,' says James.

James is a grey haired man in his fifties. He is wearing black corduroy trousers and a navy blue v-neck pullover on top of a white shirt and tie. Somehow James does not look like the sort of person I would expect to find on the seminar.

'I heard that it finishes late and I came on the bus and the last one leaves at ten thirty.'

'We will organise the logistics of lifts and getting people home later,' says Kim. 'Thank you James.'

James sits and we acknowledge him with our clapping.

'I am going to go through the agreements that you have made.'

Kim goes through the set of rules that we have already agreed to accept. They are:

For the twelve day duration of the seminar - No alcohol. No non-prescribed or recreational drugs. No headache relief drugs such as paracetamol and aspirin.

During the training - Be on time. No nicotine replacement aids whilst inside the training room. Keep our name badges on. Do not leave the room unless directed by a trainer. Do not speak in the room unless sharing or directed to do so by a trainer. To stay seated unless sharing or directed otherwise. To leave all bags, watches, cigarettes, food and drink at the back of the room. Not to bring any recording equipment into the room. Not to sit in the same seat after each break.

'There is one more,' says Kim. 'You may not sit next to anyone that you know or anyone that you have sat next to before. Is anyone sitting next to someone they know?'

A couple of hands go up and they are directed to different seats.

'Yes Helen.'

Helen is a stout girl with curly, shoulder length ginger hair. She is wearing a dress that resembles a long smock. She looks like she might have just brought a pale of milk into the farmhouse kitchen.

'I met Celia last Wednesday. Does that count?'

'Did you know her before the seminar?' Kim asks.

21

'No.'

'You may sit next to her now but not again.'

Kim waits for a couple of seconds after Helen has sat down.

'I'm not going to keep reminding you to acknowledge the person who has spoken or shared,' she says.

(Applause for Helen)

'Why do we have to have these agreements?' asks Anthony. 'They seem a bit trivial to me.'

Anthony has a round face with plump cheeks. He looks to be in his early thirties. He is wearing beige cotton trousers and a black pullover.

'Agreements always seem trivial to people who don't keep agreements,' says Kim.

(Laughter)

'They are essential to the working of the seminar. It may become evident to you later.'

(Applause)

A few more people ask other questions, for example, about food breaks or can they get a drink if they are thirsty. Kim tells them that they will be able to refresh themselves when they have been told they can have a break.

While these questions and answers are going backwards and forwards four of the trainers hand out small notebooks and pencils. These are passed along the rows from the end. Kim steps down from the stage and walks to the space between the two blocks of chairs.

'These notebooks and pencils that you have been given are special notebooks and pencils,' she says. 'They are special because they are enlightenment notebooks and pencils. They are enlightenment notebooks and pencils because they have special properties, one of which is that they cannot be lost or forgotten. They can only be thrown away or maliciously discarded. Because of this they are very expensive. If you throw them away, or maliciously discard them you will have to pay to have them replaced. The notebooks are ten pounds and the pencils are five pounds. You will be using them to make notes at various points throughout the seminar. Yes Snick,' says Kim.

She peers at Snick's name badge.

'I'm terrible for forgetting things,' says Snick.

Snick has a Welsh accent He has collar-length reddish hair and wears a grey-blue cotton shirt with red cotton trousers.

'Always leaving things lying around I am.'

'You can't leave these lying around. These are enlightenment notebooks and pencils. They cannot be left lying around.'

There are a few chuckles as Snick sits down.

(Applause)

Kim then explains that we will undergo a number of processes during the seminar. The first of these is one in which we stand and go to the space behind the blocks of seats. There we are told to pick someone out (starting with the person next to us), make eye contact and say hello to the name on their badge. The other person responds in the same manner. We then hold eye contact with that person for thirty seconds before moving on to someone else. Kim says that we should try and make a connection with that person. I notice that some people are uncomfortable with the eye contact and blush or fidget their eyes away early. One person named Martin has something around his eyelashes like a sort of crust. This, accompanied by a somewhat disturbing look in his eye, unnerves me slightly.

23

We return to our seats and there follows a period of sharing in which we are encouraged to share what we experienced during the process.

'Yes Marjory.'

Kim picks out a woman who is short, in her forties, dressed in a tweed skirt and cardigan but with a psychedelic coloured blouse underneath. Marjory looks like a rock and roll librarian.

'I really enjoyed that. I felt like I made a connection with some people, although I felt some others were holding back.'

'Thank you Marjory.'

(Applause)

'Yes Brian.'

Brian is short, around five feet six or seven and stocky. He is in his late twenties but his hair is receding prematurely. He speaks in a bristling almost aggressive manner.

'Were we supposed to feel something? I didn't feel anything. I just looked at their eyes and said hello.'

Brian sits down.

'Stand up Brian. Don't sit until I have answered your question or until you've finished sharing.'

Brian stands up again.

'You're not supposed to feel anything,' continues Kim. 'We are just trying to get you to loosen up. We want you to unclench your buttocks a little.'

(Laughter)

'It's going to be a long day and a long seminar so we don't want you tiring yourselves out being uptight. Thank you Brian.'

Brian sits down with a frown.

(Applause)

'Yes Tania.'

Tania is young and thin with long, straight, blonde hair and big blue eyes. She looks like the youngest girl in the room. She is dressed in jeans, a floppy muslin shirt and a loose waistcoat in a similar material.

'I didn't like it at first. I'm not used to looking people directly in the eye so I was nervous at first, then I got into it. I'm going to start to always look people in the eye when I speak to them now.'

'Thank you Tania.'

(Applause)

'I found it easy,' says Pat.

Pat is a tall young man, probably mid twenties. He is wearing blue jeans and a blue stripped shirt. He is well spoken. He looks like an estate agent on his day off.

'In my line of work I speak to people every day. I always look them in the eye.'

'And what is your line of work?' asks Kim.

'I've just qualified as a teacher,' he says.

(Applause)

And so it goes on for what seems like more than an hour, although with the clocks taped over and not having a watch, it is hard to tell. I am surprised at how the trainees not only share about what they felt during the introduction process but also on a variety of other seemingly unrelated subjects. One person manages to go completely off the subject, going into detail about his journey to the hotel this morning.

When Kim brings the sharing to an end she gets us to sit with our eyes closed for a few minutes. The room is quiet except for the sound of breathing and the odd cough and sniff.

'Open your eyes and pay attention.'

Kim says that today is a day in which the trainees get to know each other. She speaks to us about the pace of the seminar. She says that it is dependent on us. If we are slow the seminar will be slow.

'No hiding,' she says. 'Everyone must get involved in sharing. As long as you keep your backsides in the room you will all *get it* by the time the seminar is finished.'

A few hands go up but Kim tells them to wait and then goes on to re-iterate the importance of keeping our agreements.

'If you keep your agreements and stay in the room you will *get it*,' she says. 'Even if you sleep right through it, you will *get it*.'

Kim then tells us that, during the seminar, we will be using words and phrases that have concepts attached to them. She says that there is a certain amount of folly attached to words and their meanings.

'Words don't always convey the appropriate sentiment. We will be pointing out these words and phrases and making sure that we are all clear about what we mean by them. We are, in essence, going to get you communicating. Something you will hear during the seminar is the term to *get it*. Does anyone know what *getting it* means? Yes Karen.'

'To understand,' says Karen.

Karen looks like she is in her early forties but is probably younger. She clears her throat after she speaks like she has a smoker's cough.

'Yes,' says Kim. 'The dictionary meaning is to obtain, acquire, receive, catch, cause to be, generate, communicate, to understand.'

(Applause for Karen)

'Is it to be enlightened,' offers Sam.

Sam is a fair haired man in his twenties with a Yorkshire accent.

'I was told that we get enlightened. Is that what *getting it* is?'

'You'll know what *getting it* is when you get it,' says Kim.

(Applause)

'It's said that we will be enlightened at the end of this seminar. Does that mean we'll understand the meaning of life?'

This is Sylvie, a nice looking woman with short mouse coloured hair and an impish grin.

'Stay in the room Sylvie and you'll certainly *get* the meaning of *your* life,' replies Kim.

(Applause for Sylvie)

'Someone told me that we get brainwashed on this seminar.'

It is a male voice from the back of the room. I can't see who it is.

'No, what happens is you get un-brainwashed,' says Kim.

'Is it called the Exegesis programme because we get re-programmed?' asks Sylvie.

'No it's called the Exegesis programme because you get de-programmed,' replies Kim. 'The important thing is, if you keep you backside in the room you will *get it*.'

There follows some sharing about the different meanings and connotations surrounding the phrase *'getting it'*. Each sharing is acknowledged by applause as the sharer sits. It has become automatic now.

A few people earnestly ask questions. It is as if they are seeking advanced notice of what will happen on the seminar. Others seem to be content to allow the seminar to run its own course without drawing any conclusions.

'What is going to happen over the next five days and is there

27

anything we should do?' asks Mal.

Mal is a big man. Around six feet four inches tall and heavily set. His size is exacerbated by the chunky pullover he is wearing. His voice has a slight West Country burr.

'What is going to happen over the next five days is that you are going to be made to do everything that you have been trying not to do all of your lives.'

Kim walks towards where Mal is standing.

'You are going to experience fear, anger, apathy and some things that you didn't even know you have been avoiding experiencing.'

'Is there anything we should do though?' asks Mal.

'Nothing,' says Kim. 'Do nothing. Although I know that you are all going to do everything you can to avoid your experience. You're going to fall asleep, get hungry, you'll want to pee, want to smoke. You are going to do whatever your reasonable mind normally does to stop you from living, to stop you from experiencing. You are going to break your agreements, moan and generally hate being in this room.'

(Applause for Mal)

Kim smiles a wry smile.

'But it will not do you any good because if you keep your foot in the room, at the end of the seminar, you will get it.'

Looking around I see some of the trainees still look anxious. Some shift around on their chairs. I am aware of my empty stomach and my aching backside. I wonder if everyone will get through this. We have only been in the room for, what must be, three hours. I knew it was going to be difficult but this is starting off harder than I had imagined.

After what must be another hour of sharing, Kim says we can

have a break for forty five minutes. I am surprised when she says that it is two fifteen. We have been in the room for over five hours without a break.

'Back by three,' she says.

We exit the room. Some of the trainees go straight to the lavatory, some go outside to smoke a cigarette, some, like me, head off to get something to eat. At the delicatessen cafe around the corner I eat a sandwich and drink some water. I sit next to two other trainees: Tania and Sarah. They tell me that they are friends and that they decided to do the seminar together after Sarah's brother did it. Sarah looks like a brunette version of Tania.

'Sarah's brother changed completely,' says Tania. 'He's older than us but he always seemed immature. Now he's grown up. He's got so much energy and confidence as well.'

I say that I had noticed a huge positive change in the person who got me to do it.

Sarah says that she doesn't know what's going to happen but she knows it will be incredible. Tania agrees and nods her head in approval. I say that I hope it will be incredible too, before heading back.

At the hotel I nod to a couple of people smoking a last cigarette outside and head for the lavatory. I relieve myself, then wash my hands and face in cold water. I think to myself that, tomorrow, I must bring a toothbrush, toothpaste and a hand towel. Staying as fresh as possible will help me get through the long sessions.

I walk into the room just behind Tania and Sarah. As we enter we are, as before, handed our name tags and relieved of our bags, coats and watches. We are a few minutes early. Inside the room half of the trainees are already seated. The rest hurry in over the following minutes. No one is late.

Kim enters the room and reminds us not to sit next to anyone we know or have sat next to previously. There is some swapping of chairs and chatter and laughter as Kim looks on with a frown.

'You have agreed not to talk whilst you are in the room unless directed to do so,' she says. 'If you are unable to keep to your agreements you will be asked to leave.'

The room falls silent.

'You are going to get the chance to come up here and tell everyone who you are and what you want to get from the seminar,' continues Kim. 'Because there are so many of you I want to have three people waiting to come up on the stage at all times. We need to get a production line going or we will be here until tomorrow.'

Two of the stern looking trainers from the back come and assist in manoeuvring the trainees into a line at the side of the stage. I am immediately apprehensive about standing up and speaking in front of one hundred and thirty people. I am sure that I am not the only one feeling this.

First up is Jed. He is dressed in jeans and a shirt without a collar.

'My name is Jed. I am here because I want to change my job.'

'What is your job?' asks Kim.

'I'm a salesman and I hate it,' says Jed.

'Maybe, after the seminar, you'll get to love your job or maybe you'll find a new one,' says Kim. 'Thank you Jed. Acknowledge him,' she says in a stern voice when we forget to clap.

We all applaud quickly and loudly.

'Next,' says Kim.

'Hello my name is Brian and I don't know why I'm here.'

(Laughter)

'You're here because you chose to be here,' says Kim.

Kim is not laughing. In fact she looks irritated.

'What do you want to get out of the seminar?'

'I don't know. I only agreed to do it because my fiancé wanted me to. She did it last month and wanted me to do it. She said it would improve our relationship.'

Brian follows this with a little laugh.

'So you want to improve your relationship with you fiancé then,' says Kim. 'That is why you chose to be here.'

'Well yes.'

Brian shrugs as he speaks.

'Then why not say so instead of being a big pussy about it? Take responsibility. You chose to do it not your fiancée. But there you go! If you fuck up you can always shift the blame onto her. Next,' says Kim.

(Applause)

Brian steps down from the stage. There is some laughter as well as the applause. To me, Brian looks a little red in the face. I notice that a few people look surprised at Kim's directness. The person sitting next to me, a girl with the name 'Gail' written on her name tag, turns to me. Her face carries an expression of terrified apprehension.

'H hi, muh muh my nuh nuh name i i is Greg,' the next person up on stage stutters. 'Uh uh uh I am here to i i improve muh muh my stuh stuh stutter and guh guh gain more cah confidence.'

'Stay in the room Greg. I guarantee that, by the end of the seminar, we'll have you bullshitting like the rest of us with no stutter,' says Kim.

There is a burst of nervous laughter and applause.

'My name is Simon and I want to rid myself of the feeling that I am better than or superior to everyone else.'

Simon is tall and slender. He looks to be in his early fifties. He is wearing creased, grey trousers and an elbow patched tweed jacket that has seen better days. Like James, Simon is not the sort of person you might expect to be doing the seminar. I am starting to realize that there are a variety of different types of people here.

'Maybe you'll find out that you actually are superior to everyone else,' says Kim.

(Applause and some laughter)

One after one the trainees come up to the stage and say what they want to gain from the seminar. Kim's response, questions and interaction probably takes between two and five minutes. I make a quick calculation. One hundred and thirty people at an average of three minutes each is six and a half hours; four minutes each is more than eight and a half hours.

'We are going to be here forever,' I think to myself and indeed it begins to feel like forever as the trainees come up one after another.

'My name is Kate. I am an actor and I am here to see if this course will develop my skills. A friend of mine did it and he said that by knowing himself he was able to express his characters so much better.'

Kate is short and blonde and prettily made up. She is wearing a loose jumper that shows a bit of her shoulder. She is wearing leggings with long thick socks. She looks like she's just taken a break from a rehearsal to be here.

'How long have you been an actor?' asks Kim.

'Two years.'

'Have you had much work?'

'I appeared in the Cherry Orchard. It ran at the Yvonne Arnaud theatre in Farnham. But I haven't had much since.'

'Have you tried for many parts?'

'Yes. Quite a few.'

Kate blushes slightly like she is ashamed to own up to the fact.

'Well maybe it's your sales and presentation skills that need improving rather than your acting. Then you might get more work.'

(Applause for Kate)

And on it goes. The trainees climb up on to the stage and state their goals. I wonder what the purpose of all this is. Is it being done to create a feeling of tedium and why? The other trainees look tired, agitated, irritated and bored. Some yawn and stretch. A woman sitting next to me, whose name tag reads 'Julia', keeps raising herself from her seat by an inch or so with her hands. To relive her aching backside I assume. She smiles at me when I notice.

'My name is Amanda and I have had a difficult two years because of illness.'

Amanda is thin, she wears spectacles and has medium length hair tied back. Her voice is quiet and timid.

'Can't hear,' someone shouts and Amanda clears her throat with a little cough and speaks louder. Not much louder but just enough to hear if you strain.

'I have felt tired and unable to concentrate and,'

Kim interrupts. 'What is the illness?' she asks. 'There is nothing in your questionnaire about it.'

'I don't know what is wrong,' says Amanda. 'For the last two

33

years I haven't felt right.'

'But have you been to the doctor? Has there been a diagnosis?'

'They can't find anything. They think it could be depression but I don't feel depressed, just tired.'

The exchange goes backwards and forwards for several minutes. I am aware of a growing irritability amongst some of the trainees who probably feel, like I do, that this is taking too long.

'Are you receiving any medication?' asks Kim.

'No.'

'Then perhaps you are here to re-energise yourself,' says Kim. 'One way or the other I'm sure we'll get to the bottom of your racket. Next.'

Kim cuts a frowning Amanda off and moves on. Amanda receives a less than enthusiastic round of applause and Kim admonishes us and tells us to acknowledge and support our fellow trainees whether we empathise or agree with them or not.

Finally, after what seems like hours, Kim, to everyone's' relief, declares that we are to have a break for one and a half hours.

Once again, the trainees head for the exit and do the same things that they did at the earlier break. It is seven o'clock in the evening.

Two other trainees, Snick and Brian, ask me if I'm going to eat and we go to a chain pasta restaurant near the hotel in Praed Street.

'I'm not sure if this is bollocks or not,' says Brian.

'I don't think it's got going yet,' I reply.

'A mate of mine has done the EST seminar as well as this one and he reckons they are both great,' says Snick.

'What the fuck is EST?' asks Brian.

'EST stands for Erhard Seminar Training. It's the same as this.

34

They lock you in a room and call you an arsehole and make you get in touch with what you are experiencing. It's been going in the States for years. It's massive out there. This mate of mine like, he's a seminar junkie. He does all these courses. Reckons this one is the best now.'

'So when will they start to call us arseholes?' asks Brian.

'Tomorrow probably,' replies Snick. 'That Kim's a bit of alright though,' he adds laughing.

I arrive back in the room at eight twenty five and go through the routine of handing in my stuff and picking up my name tag. Once again half of the delegates are already seated. No one is late. The process of introductions continues.

'My name is Kenny and I'm here to get myself ready to go into business on my own.'

Kenny is Afro-Caribbean. He is well spoken with a London accent. He wears jeans and a v-neck pullover with a polo shirt underneath. His clothes look like they have designer labels.

'What do you do now?' asks Kim.

'I'm a salesman,' he says. 'I sell sports goods.'

'What business do you want to start?'

'I don't know. I'm looking out for opportunities.'

'Are you up for finishing this seminar?'

'Yes.'

'Then you won't have a problem getting your business together.'

(Applause)

The introductions go on. Some people like Kenny, have no

problem getting up and speaking in front of the room. Some are nervous and Kim has to coax them through the ordeal.

After several more hours I am tired. Carl, one of the people sitting next to me, raises his eyebrows and gives me a supportive nod as I shift in my seat to relieve my aching behind. Looking around I see that one or two people have nodded off to sleep. They look like they have assumed the crash position in an aircraft, leaning forward with their heads down over their knees. Others shift uncomfortably in their seats like me. Some stretch and yawn. A few look quite distressed.

'My name is Claire and I am here to try and improve my relationship with my boyfriend.'

Claire has dark hair and light, white skin that is almost translucent. She is wearing a knee length blue skirt with a t-shirt and cardigan.

'What is wrong with your relationship now?' asks Kim.

'Nothing. It is just that my boyfriend has asked me to marry him and I'm not sure.'

'If you are not sure then the answer is probably, no,' says Kim. 'Stay in the room and you will be able to make up your mind by the end.'

(Applause)

Thankfully, the introductions come to an end. When the last person sits down the applause is more out of relief rather than acknowledgement of the trainee.

Kim spends another half an hour or so going over our agreements and then deals with the logistics of getting everyone home. I agree to drop Jed in Hammersmith and Marjory in Chiswick on my way home.

Finally we are allowed to leave. Once again people dash to the lavatories. Some light up outside the hotel. Marjory smokes a hand rolled cigarette on the way to the car. It is a quarter to one on the Saturday morning.

'Fuck, that was tedious,' says Jed.

Marjory laughs.

'Kim intimated that it's all part of the process. The tedium, boredom and the sore bum are designed to do something,' I say.

'Any idea what?' asks Marjory.

'Not yet,' I say.

First Saturday

It is easier getting to and parking near the hotel on the Saturday. I head inside past the last minute smokers and on into the room. I am with Jed and Marjory who I agreed to pick up on my way in.

Once again the trainers relieve everyone of their bags, watches and paraphernalia. They give me my name badge and check me through. Their facial expressions remain disturbingly neutral.

I take a seat in the left hand block, in the middle of the fifth row from the front. The trainers assume the same positions as the day before: some sitting at the side, the rest at the back and a couple outside the door. In the same way as the day before someone enters the room and walks to the front and onto the low stage. This time, however, the person is a man. He is wearing a well cut suit, white shirt and tie. As he walks along the row of seats he says, 'Good morning.'

A few people respond with a half hearted, 'Good morning.'

'Not very energised,' I hear him say, almost under his breath.

I note that everyone's eyes are fixed on him. Even though he is rather heavily set there is a charismatic grace and purpose about his movements. His skin is brown but not like you would get from a suntan. He has a strong aquiline nose and pronounced nostrils. Strangely, or maybe not, he looks almost guru like. I wonder if he is part Indian.

'My name is Robert,' he says. 'I am here to ensure that you *get it*. You are here because you are arseholes and your lives are a mess. You have all said what you want to get out of the seminar but basically you are here because you are arseholes and your lives don't work.'

Robert is standing by the lectern looking along the rows of seats, at us trainees.

'First, I want you arseholes to take out your enlightenment notebooks and pencils.'

He waits for a few seconds.

'Has everyone got them out?'

A couple of hands go up.

'Yes Jules.'

Jules is a girl, probably in her late twenties. She has short hair and a round face with red cheeks.

'I forgot to bring mine,' she says. 'I left it on my bedside table.'

'They are enlightenment notebooks and pencils,' replies Robert. 'They cannot be forgotten or lost or left behind. You have maliciously disposed of yours like a typical arsehole.'

'No really,' says Jules I left them behind by mistake. I was in a hurry this morning I didn't want to be late.'

'They cannot be left behind by mistake. They are enlightenment notebooks and pencils. You will be charged for their replacement. Thank you Jules.'

(Applause)

'Yes Dan.'

'I'm sorry, I've lost mine. I wasn't going to say but I feel I have to. I must have left it on the bus. I've still got the pencil though,' he says.

(Laughter)

'Typical arsehole. You have maliciously thrown it away,' says Robert. 'You will be charged for the replacement.'

(Applause for Dan)

A trainer hands out new notebooks to those who have forgotten or misplaced theirs.

'I want you arseholes to write down what you got from yesterday's introductions and statements of what you want to achieve. We'll see what your goals look like at the end of the programme.'

Robert walks slowly to one end of the stage. He is looking intently at the trainees. He turns and walks back.

'During this seminar we are going to explore your arseholeness and see it for what it is,' he says.

'Yes Jen.'

Jen is a woman in her fifties. She has grey hair, watery blue eyes and a plum polo neck pullover.

'Why are we arseholes?' she asks with a smile.

'You are arseholes because you avoid your experience and you are laden with beliefs. You do everything you can to avoid your experience and cling on to your shitty beliefs. During this seminar you are going to do everything you can to avoid your experience. You are going to do everything you can to cling to your beliefs but nothing you do will help you because if you keep your foot in the room you will *get it*. By the end of the seminar you will certainly have acknowledged your experience, probably for the first time and we may even get you to chip away at a few of those beliefs. Right now you are stuck with your beliefs. They are part of you. You nurture them, you cling to them. All the little rackets that you believe will work for you in your lives but really just hold you back. Like Jules' little racket of leaving stuff behind and Dan's racket of losing things. Dan believes that losing stuff and being scatty makes him endearing and loveable but it doesn't. It just makes him another arsehole.'

(Laughter)

Dan is sitting a couple of rows in front of me. His ears have gone red.

'What I want you arseholes to do is to drop your beliefs for this seminar. I don't want you to believe anything I say or anything that goes on.'

(Applause for Jen)

'What should we believe then?' asks Jules.

'Nothing. Not a thing.'

'But we have to believe something.'

'No you don't,' says Robert. 'One thing that you are going to find out is that you arseholes don't *need* to believe anything. Stop believing and start experiencing.'

(Applause for Jules)

'We shouldn't believe anything you say then,' says Martin.

Martin is the young man with the odd stare and the crust around his eyes. He has a waver in his voice like he is about to break down in tears at any moment.

'That's right.'

'Including that?'

'Including that,' Robert replies.

Martin blinks his eyes. His voice goes higher in tone as he speaks.

'That's silly.'

'Yes. But let's be silly,' says Robert. 'You're all arseholes anyway. A little silliness will do you the world of good. Let's be silly and drop our beliefs and start to experience what we are getting. Thank you Martin.'

(Applause)

'Aren't our beliefs just instinctive though,' says Jerry.

41

Jerry must be in his early thirties. He has a face that looks like it is always ready to smile. I had nodded to him a couple of times as I passed him at the front of the hotel. He is one of the smokers.

'They are anything but instinctive,' Robert replies. 'Let us look at ourselves and how we operate. We all have basic instincts. We are born with them. These basic instincts are: to survive and procreate. Survival and procreation are the basic instincts of all living organisms. They are wired into our being. Without these basic instincts nothing would survive, nothing would evolve. Our beliefs on the other hand are acquired.'

Robert looks intently at us for a few seconds.

'Our beliefs are acquired. No one is born with a belief.' he repeats loudly.

(Applause for Jerry)

'Beliefs get in the way of our experience,' Robert continues. 'They dictate what we experience, what we *get*. Yes Paul.'

Paul is thin with short blonde hair. He has an innocent looking face and a Midlands accent.

'I don't get it,' he says. 'If you are saying that beliefs are bad then why do we have them?'

'I didn't say beliefs were bad. I didn't say they were good. I said that they got in the way of your experience.'

'But I think my beliefs are good.'

'That's because you're an arsehole. You have a belief around beliefs. You believe that some are good and some are bad. I am saying beliefs get in the way of your experience. You don't experience anything. That is why you are an arsehole.'

'I don't see how beliefs can dictate what we experience though.'

'The fact that you can't see it is part of your arseholeness. But don't worry. We are going to look at our beliefs. We are going to see

42

them for what they are.'

(Applause for Paul)

'Which one of you arseholes can give me an example of a belief that people might have?' asks Robert. 'Yes Snick.'

'Sex,' says Snick. 'People have beliefs around sex.'

'I'm not surprised *you've* brought that up,' says Robert.

(Laughter)

'So what beliefs do people have around sex?'

'Some people believe that same sex partners are wrong,' offers Snick.

'And some believe that same sex partners are OK. Thank you Snick,' says Robert.

(Applause)

'But the people who believe that being gay is wrong, are themselves wrong,' says Paul.

'That is your belief,' Robert replies. 'We are not making a judgement on whether the beliefs are good or bad we are just identifying what they are.'

'But there are good beliefs and bad beliefs. Like, killing is wrong and saving life is right,' says Paul.

Paul is standing nonchalantly with a hand in one of his pockets.

'They are still just beliefs. It could be argued that in some instances killing is the right thing to do. Are there any meat eaters here who like to eat their animals alive?'

(Some laughter)

'I meant killing people,' says Paul.

'So, do you have a belief that it is not OK to kill people but OK to kill animals?' asks Robert.

'No, I mean that some beliefs are right and some are wrong.'

'And I mean that, that is your belief, a belief not everyone necessarily shares. Thank you Paul.'

(Applause)

'Let's have some more examples of beliefs.'

'Sex with animals. Some believe that sex with animals is good,' says Lisa.

Lisa is small. She has dark hair and skin that looks like it would tan easily but hasn't seen the sun for a while.

'We've got an odd bunch in this time,' says Robert.

He looks around at the trainees with an expression of a man who has just realized he is the only sane person in a room full of lunatics. This elicits a burst of laughter from most of the trainees.

'Some people believe that sex with animals is wrong, some believe it's OK. Thank you Lisa. Yes Melinda.'

(Applause for Lisa)

Melinda is what you might call, a well turned out and well spoken girl. She has streaked blonde hair and a ski tan. She is almost the opposite in looks to Lisa.

'Sex with animals *is* wrong,' she says.

'Fine,' says Robert. 'That's your belief.'

'No, it is wrong,' replies Melinda.

Her voice gets a little shrill.

'That's your belief,' says Robert. 'How do you know, when someone has their penis rammed up a pig, that the pig isn't enjoying it? Has anyone asked the pig?'

(Laughter from some of the trainees. A few others look on disapprovingly)

'Thank you Melinda.'

(Applause)

'So people have beliefs around sex and sexuality. They have beliefs around morals and behaviour as well it seems.'

Robert goes back up on to the stage and stands looking down at the first row of trainees.

'Come on, let's have some more beliefs.'

People raise their hands and are picked. They speak, sit down and we acknowledge them.

'Race. Some people believe that some races are superior and some inferior.'

'Aliens from outer space.'

'Manners. Some people believe that manners are not important.'

'Some believe that manners are important,' adds Robert.

'God, people believe in God,' someone says.

'And some people believe God doesn't exist.'

'Ghosts,' suggests another.

After a number of offerings Robert raises his hand in a 'stop' gesture.

'Ok,' he says. 'What is a belief?'

He walks to the lectern and reads from a set of notes.

'The dictionary explanation of a belief is: confidence, trust or faith. An acceptance of something to be real or true, a convinced opinion. Religious doctrine, a creed. A considered view, a judgement.'

He walks to the edge of the stage and stands in front of the lectern.

'So we know that you have beliefs. We know you don't all have the same beliefs around the same things. So where do we get these beliefs?'

No hands go up. Robert, once again, gets down from the stage and walks to the aisle between the two blocks of chairs.

'There are a few of you arseholes hiding out there. Some of you arseholes don't want to share. You think you can get through this without offering anything. You think you can get a free ride on everyone else's energy. Energy burglars, I know who you are. If I have to start picking people I will.'

Hands go up immediately.

'Yes Carol. Where do people get their beliefs from?'

Carol stands up. She is very nervous. She is wearing a jumper with a floppy neck, a black skirt and boots. Her look of terror increases.

'From our parents?' she asks timidly.

'Can't hear!' someone shouts.

'From our parents,' she says louder.

'Yes,' says Robert. 'From our parents. That's one of the first places that people pick up beliefs from. Thank you Carol.'

Carol sits to enthusiastic acknowledgement. She is beaming like she has just won a prize. It was clearly difficult for her to stand and speak in front of a large group of people. I try and recall if she had a similar problem yesterday, during the introductions, but I can't remember.

'What sort of beliefs did you get from your parents?' Robert asks.

He waives his hand outwards to indicate that it is an open question.

'Yes Sally.'

Sally stands. She is olive skinned with dark hair that curls up in two flicks at the side of her cheeks. She shakes the flicks away from her face as she speaks.

'My parents were very strict. They taught me the difference

46

between right and wrong. They made sure that we knew how to behave,' she says.

Sally nods her head as if she is agreeing with herself.

'Give me an example,' says Robert.

'Well, for example. Be considerate to others.'

'Was that a right or a wrong?' asks Robert.

'A right of course.'

Sally shakes her head and looks indignant that Robert should ask.

'Just asking,' says Robert.

(Applause for Sally)

'Have you noticed how many beliefs are to do with right and wrong? Most of the examples that you have offered up in fact. Is that interesting?'

Robert waits for a few seconds.

'Obviously not,' he remarks. 'This is going to be like getting blood out of a stone.'

People continue to offer up examples of where we might get our beliefs from:

'Upbringing'

'Teachers'

'The Church, religion'

'Friends, peers'

'Society'

After each sharing we acknowledge the person sharing by clapping. It is interesting how it becomes an automatic response, like Pavlov's dogs. I am surprised that, during the sharing, there are so many disagreements about beliefs. There is further dissimilarity when some

47

people want to add something or comment about what has been said.

'Surely it is preferable to have a belief system based on moral judgement. Isn't one of the problems in the world because people can't see the difference between right and wrong?' says Martin.

Martin is standing. He is blinking his eyes as he speaks. He definitely has a problem with his eyes.

'No,' Robert replies. 'It doesn't work. One man's right isn't the same as another man's. The Klu Klux Clan member who's just killed the black man thinks he's right. He's a reasonable guy. He might work at the bank in the day. Good old Jack, pillar of the community, but in the evening he's got his white sheet on and his pointy hat and he's out chasing black people off the streets because he believes he is right.'

'But he is wrong,' says Martin. 'If he had a belief that says black people were equal he wouldn't murder or oppress or whatever.'

'And how exactly do you change good ol' Jack's belief then?' asks Robert.

'I don't know,' says Martin. 'Education?'

'No! Experience,' says Robert. 'What if Jack went and lived with a black family and experienced their way of life. Experienced who they were and what they were like. Jack would be experiencing not believing. If people stopped believing and started to experience, then we might start to get somewhere.'

(Applause for Martin)

'Martin's view is just as dictatorial as good 'ol Jack's if you think about it,' says Grant.

Grant is a young man with collar length blonde hair. He is wearing a denim jacket over a t-shirt and white cotton trousers. I can see from where I am sitting that he is wearing cowboy boots.

'You can't dictate to people what their beliefs are,' he continues.

(Applause)

Martin puts his hand up and, when picked, stands and defends his argument. Grant replies and there is a heated exchange between the two. We other trainees, of course, acknowledge Martin and Grant after each time one of them has spoken. Robert allows the discourse to go backward and forward a few times by continuing to pick them out when they raise their hands.

'See what people will do to defend their beliefs,' says Robert. 'If we'd have left that to continue a fight may have broken out.'

(Nervous laughter)

'It's easy to see how some wars start.'

Robert walks along the front of the low stage. He is looking down at us. It is as if he is scrutinising us individually, to see if we understand what is going on with regard to the discourse.

'You see?' he continues. 'Different beliefs, but each person clings to their own one. They hate to be wrong.'

The sharing continues while Robert prowls along the front of the low stage like he is waiting to pounce on somebody.

'You arseholes spend all of your lives filtering the world through your beliefs. That's one of the reasons why your lives don't work. Yesterday Jed, over there, said that he is not happy in his job.'

Robert points to Jed.

'He hates it and wants to change it. His belief tells him that changing his job will make him happy but it won't. He may get a new job but he'll spend all of his time trying to do the job in the manner his belief says it should be done. He'll never experience what it's like to really do

49

the job because his belief will get in the way. He'll end up hating that job and his belief will tell him he has to change that to be happy.'

Jed's hand goes up.

'Yes Jed.'

'So you're saying that we should stop believing?'

'Yes arsehole.'

'What should we believe then?'

'Nothing. Drop your beliefs and start experiencing.'

(Applause for Jed)

'But I still think we have to believe in something,' says Ruth.

Ruth is plump with fine white skin. She is wearing plum coloured culotte type trousers with a loose cardigan. She looks clean and scrubbed. Her hair is tied back in a short pony tail.

'That's one of your beliefs,' says Robert. 'And it's one of the reasons why you are an arsehole and your life doesn't work. You are so wrapped up in your beliefs that you never get to experience anything. It's the same for all of you. That's why you're arseholes.'

(Applause for Ruth)

'But what should we believe?' asks Carol.

'We've been all over this before,' says Brian. 'Have you people been sleeping? We covered this an hour ago.'

Brian is not the only one who is frustrated at having to go back over issues just because a couple of people seem to have missed them. The feeling is not helped, of course, by the fact that people have sore backsides, are craving nicotine, are hungry or need to go to the lavatory.

'And why does that piss you off Brian?'

Robert walks over to the end of the row that Brian is standing in.

'Acknowledge Carol please,' Robert reminds us.

(Applause)

50

'Well?' asks Robert. 'Why does that get you angry?'

'Because I don't want to spend my time needlessly going over shit.'

'Why? Because you believe your time is valuable? We'll see what happens when you can't keep up or you fall asleep.'

'I just wanted to share that I'm irritated at having to spend time on stuff that's already been covered.'

'I get that arsehole,' says Robert. 'Christ! Someone acknowledged their experience,' he adds. 'Thank you.'

(Applause)

'Any more arseholes want to share something?' Robert asks.

'I don't believe I am an arsehole,' says Felix.

'That's what all the arseholes say,' Robert replies.

(Laughter, then applause for Felix)

Felix has a slight accent. He could be Dutch or German. He wears black plastic rimmed glasses and is dressed in a black crew neck jumper with black trousers. He is short and rotund in shape. I notice that Felix, like some others, is someone that I hadn't been aware of before. It is curious how you can be in a room with someone for 24 hours and not notice them.

'Yes Simon.'

Simon stands. He is wearing the same tweed jacket with the elbow patches. He looks like he might pull a pipe out of his pocket at any moment and start smoking it.

'Is it really necessary to keep calling everyone arseholes?' he asks.

'Yes,' says Robert.

Robert has a look on his face that says, 'of course there is'. The look is utterly hilarious and almost everyone bursts out laughing.

51

'What do you get when I call you an arsehole Simon?'

'Do you mean, how do I feel?' says Simon.

'I mean, what do you experience arsehole. But how you think you feel will do.'

Simon's face is reddening.

'Well! Rather insulted,' he says.

'You are angry!'

'Not angry, more irritated.'

'No need to try and water down your anger just to appear reasonable Simon. You are fucking angry at being called an arsehole. It pisses you off.'

'I'd rather you didn't swear.'

Simon is red in the face. I can see his bottom lip quivering.

'I don't give a flying fuck what you'd rather I did or didn't do.'

Robert leaves the stage at the side and walks to the end of the row where Simon is standing. A few of the trainees sit up in their chairs, some fidget and look distinctly uncomfortable with the confrontation.

'I don't like swearing,' says Simon.

Simon is trying to remain composed but his voice is raised.

'Why don't you like swearing Simon?' Robert asks.

'I believe that is unnecessary.'

'There you have it,' says Robert. 'Simon has a belief around swearing. He believes that it is unnecessary. When he hears swearing he gets anger. Well your anger is nothing to do with me,' he continues. 'That's what you bring to the party. You are an arsehole who gets angry when he hears swearing. There are plenty of arseholes here who don't get angry when they hear swearing. They get positively joyful when they hear the words fuck or shit or bollocks.'

(Laughter from, not all but some of, the trainees)

'See!' says Robert. 'Joy! That's what those arseholes bring to the party.'

(More laughter)

'Their belief is different. When they get called an arsehole or hear swearing that don't get the same as you. They don't get anger. They're not better or worse than you they've just got different belief systems around swearing and arseholes.'

(Laughter)

'Thank you Simon.'

Simon sits. He looks a little bewildered. There is loud acknowledgement. More out of relief, I suspect, at the ending of the confrontation.

'I believe that my arse hurts,' says Brian.

(Laughter)

'No,' says Robert. 'The ache in your backside is real. Your belief might tell you that it's good or bad, fair or unfair, pleasant or unpleasant but it is real.'

'Well I believe it's unpleasant,' says Brian.

(Laughter)

'If you, really pay attention to your experience of your sore backside, go with it, explore it and truly experience it you may find that it transforms into something else.'

'Like what?' asks Brian.

'Like you not being an arsehole,' replies Robert.

(More laughter and applause for Brian)

'Look,' says Robert. 'I've been calling you all arseholes. Make a note of what you get when I call you an arsehole. Simon over there didn't like it. He got anger. Marjory over there laughed. She got amusement. Snick over there giggled like a schoolgirl. He got titillation.'

(Laughter)

'Whatever you get, hatred, fear, shame, resentment, anger, amusement; that is what you add to it. When I call you an arsehole just observe it. I'm just speaking the word, the rest is what you bring to the party, your creation. It is your beliefs that determine what emotion you get when I call you an arsehole.'

'I'm always surprised at how many people really dislike the word cunt,' says Harry. 'I mean, it's just a word.'

Harry looks to be in his early twenties. He has an impish face and darkish blonde hair.

(Applause)

'The word is insulting to women,' says Sally. 'To have a derogatory term that applies to a part of a woman's anatomy is unpleasant.'

(Applause)

'What about prick then? That's just the same,' says Harry.

(Applause)

'Prick isn't so bad,' replies Sally. 'The other word is aggressive and unpleasant.'

(Applause)

I am really impressed by the way in which Robert deals with the responses, questions and objections. No matter how seemingly trivial or irritating they are, he gives the person sharing his full attention. He appears to have an intimate understanding of the emotion and sentiment behind the words. He moves around with an energetic grace. He appears to be as fresh as when he first entered the room. When I look round at the trainers sitting at the side and to the rear, their faces are always the same: neutral and expressionless. They sit like statues, looking like they just sat down two minutes ago. On the other hand we, the trainees, look like we have been in the room for hours, which of course we have. Some are bent over with their elbows on their knees and their heads resting on their cupped hands. Some are fidgeting and shifting from buttock to buttock in an attempt to alleviate their sore backsides. Some arch their backs whilst seated, trying to stretch the aching from their torsos. We are tired and hungry. Some crave nicotine others are thinking about their bladders and wondering if they can hang on until the break, whenever that may come. I notice one person nodding off into semi-consciousness then awaking with a shake of their head.

'I am searching for the truth. For a way to improve myself,' says Mac.

Mac is a tall athletic looking young man with an outdoors complexion and a five o'clock shadow.

'And I believe that I'll know when I've found it.'

'Bull Shit,' says Robert.

Mac looks shocked at Robert's response.

'As long as you have the belief that you'll find the truth you'll never find it. You wouldn't know the truth if it came up and kicked you in the arse. An arsehole kicked in the arse, imagine that.'

Robert smiles vaguely to himself.

'You might already know the truth but you can't recognise it.'

'Well I think that I would know. I'm quite enlightened in many ways. I have attended a retreat and had conversations with Buddhist monks. I understand what you're saying about beliefs and I agree to an extent.'

'You can never experience the truth or enlightenment or whatever you want to call it whilst you have a belief about what it might be.'

Mac sits.

(Applause)

'I'll tell you a story,' Robert continues. 'There was a man who, like many others, was seeking peace of mind and everlasting happiness. He hears of a Guru who lives in a cave at the foot of the Himalayas. The Guru is said to know the secret of peace of mind and everlasting happiness so the man decides to find him. After a long search and an arduous journey he arrives at the Guru's cave and introduces himself.

"Guru, I have come in search of the secret of peace of mind and everlasting happiness."

The Guru looks at the man.

"First you must go to a monastery in Tibet and spend one year in contemplation. After one year, return and, if you are ready, I will reveal the secret."

The man agrees and spends a year in Tibet contemplating the question. After another long trek he arrives back at the Guru's cave.

"Guru, I have spent a year at the monastery in contemplation. Once again, I come in search of the answer to the secret of peace of mind and everlasting happiness."

"You are not quite ready," says the Guru. "You must go and spend a year at an Ashram in India and contemplate the question further."

The man agrees and spends a year in India studying at an Ashram. Once again he returns to the cave and presents himself to the Guru.

"Guru, I have spent a year of thought and contemplation at the Ashram."

"You are nearly ready for the answer," says the Guru. "Finally though, you must spend a year at a centre for meditation in your home

56

country. During this time you must contemplate the question further."

The man agrees and spends another year contemplating the question. He returns to the Guru.

"I have spent a year in meditation and contemplation in my own country. Surely I am ready now."

"Yes," says the Guru. "You are ready."

The man fills his chest with air in anticipation of the answer.

"The secret of peace of mind and everlasting happiness is to never argue with anyone," states the Guru.

The man looks bemused.

"That's not the secret of peace of mind and everlasting happiness," he says.

"Ok, so it isn't," says the Guru.'

Some of the trainees laugh, a few don't get it.

'You are never going to find what you are looking for while you have a belief around it.'

Robert steps back onto the low stage.

'We are going to take a short break,' Robert announces.

There is a collective sigh of relief from the trainees.

'But first we are going to do a process.'

The sigh turns to a groan.

'Under your seat is an empty box. Does everybody have one?'

Robert then asks us to inspect the box. The box is the size of a matchbox. It has a flap to open it like a playing card box. Robert asks us to imagine ourselves to be inside the little box.

'I am going to call on you by name and without opening your eyes or standing I want you to describe what it's like in your box. You do not need to acknowledge the person. Just stay in your own box. Fran.'

I hear Fran's voice describe her box.

'It's dark in here,' she says. 'The walls and corners of the box are smooth. I can feel the corners of the box. I can smell the walls and floor. They are made up of cardboard. If I stretch up I can touch the top of the box.'

It is a very impressive description. I wonder if Robert knew she would be good at imagining herself to be in the box and had picked her on purpose to help get the ball rolling.

'Joe.'

Joe is quiet for a few moments.

'I am stretched out in my box. It is very comfortable. I can touch the two ends with my hands and feet. It smells of cardboard. It is dark and I can feel the opening flap,' he says. 'I can hear people outside of my box. I can hear them breathing.'

The descriptions go on for what seems like more than an hour. Some are inventive and some less so. I wonder if the ability to visualize being in a small cardboard box says anything about the personality.

'Cath.'

'I don't like it in here. It is claustrophobic and dark. It feels cramped and I can't get comfortable. I can smell sulphur. It is unpleasant.'

Finally, Robert calls the proceeding to a halt. He has us stand up and stretch, then sit down again. We are let out for a forty five minute break. It is three fifteen in the afternoon. As usual, everyone busies themselves doing what they need to do in the short amount of time allowed. I have time for a sandwich and a visit to the lavatory before hurrying back to the room.

'We have been talking about beliefs and how they affect our emotion, our experience.'

Robert is standing on the stage looking, if anything, fresher than he did this morning. The trainers are seated in their usual seats with their usual blank expressions. Once again we have been relieved of our watches, bags, overcoats and paraphernalia. We have been handed our name badges and reminded not to sit next to anyone we know or have sat next to before.

'Let me just clarify one of the reasons why your lives don't work. You all live through your beliefs. Beliefs around whether something is good or bad. Beliefs around how something should be done. Beliefs around religion. Beliefs around sex. Beliefs around parents, friends, about everything. You all live automatically in your belief systems instead of experiencing the world as it is. Belief systems that you acquired years ago. You're stuck in your beliefs.'

Robert steps down from the stage and walks towards the centre aisle.

'If a scientist puts a mouse in a room with five boxes and places a lump of cheese in the fifth box the mouse will look in the boxes and eventually, find the cheese. How quick depends on how smelly the cheese is.'

(Some restrained laughter)

'If the scientist keeps placing the cheese in the fifth box, eventually, the mouse will learn to go straight to the fifth box. Humans will learn to do the same thing. Cheese, fifth box, that's where the cheese is. Cheese, fifth box that's where the cheese is. Now if the scientist moves the cheese to another box the mouse will still go to the fifth box to look

59

for the cheese. "Hmm! No cheese in the box." The next day he'll do the same thing, no cheese. Next day, still no cheese and so on. Eventually though, he'll look elsewhere for the cheese. The difference between humans and mice is that humans have reason and a human's reason is upheld by beliefs. The mouse doesn't have reason or beliefs. The mouse just wants the cheese. The human develops a belief around the fifth box. The human believes that the cheese belongs in the fifth box and will go to the fifth box over and over. Humans believe in the fifth box whether there is any cheese in it or not. Humans believe it is right to go to the fifth box. The human is never going to look in any other box because he knows the cheese belongs in the fifth box. The human and his reason would rather be right than get any cheese.'

Robert is standing towards the back of the aisle. Consequently, many of the trainees have to turn round in their seats to look at him.

'And your trouble is that you have too many beliefs around too many fifth boxes. And that is one of the reasons why your lives don't work. That is one of the main reasons why you are not getting any cheese.'

(Some laughter)

'And the confusing thing is that although you share many beliefs you have even more that are particular to you. You all believe in different boxes.'

Robert raises his voice.

'YOU ARE ALL LIVING IN AN UNREAL WORLD WHERE NOTHING IS THE SAME FOR ANY OF YOU. EACH OF YOU HAS A DIFFERENT VIEW OF REALITY DEPENDANT ON YOUR BELIEFS.'

Robert walks back and stands in front of the stage.

'Does everyone *get* that everyone's reality differs?' Robert asks.

60

There is a general nodding of heads in agreement.

'So what is real? Can anyone tell me what reality actually is? Yes Sylvie.'

'Consciousness. Reality is our consciousness.'

'OK. Yes Mal.'

(Applause for Sylvie)

'Everything,' he says. 'It's everything, thoughts, matter, energy, everything.'

(Applause for Mal)

'Everything that we know as individuals is what makes up our reality. All of our experiences,' says Pat.

(Applause)

'According to John Lennon, nothing is real,' says Brian.

(Laughter and applause)

'Collective consciousness,' someone says.

(Applause)

The sharing continues for more than half an hour. There are a variety of suggestions about what is reality. There are disagreements amongst the trainees as to the nature of what reality is. I hadn't thought about it before but now I have had my attention drawn to it I am surprised at how people live in the same world yet have differing views about what is real. I think that maybe this is what Robert is trying to illustrate.

'The world around us is real,' says Sally.

(Applause)

'The chair I'm sitting on is real,' says Ray. 'Everything and everyone in this room is real.'

Ray stands up. He looks to be in his mid thirties. He has thinning light coloured hair and a ruddy face like he works outside or drinks too much. It's hard to tell which.

'How do you know they are real?' asks Robert.

'Because I can see all of those things.'

'What about outside. You can't see that.'

'But I saw it earlier. I remember it. I know it will have changed slightly but intrinsically it's still there. Still the same. It exists.'

'Does everyone agree with what Ray just said?' Robert asks.

Most of the trainees nod their head in agreement a few say, 'Yes'.

'So you're saying seeing it and knowing it's there is the test of what's real? Acknowledge Ray please.'

Robert reminds us as Ray sits.

(Applause)

'Reality is what is real.' says Sam.

(Applause)

I wonder if Robert's style of presentation is one where he wants us to exhaust all of the arguments, all of the possibilities, before putting forward what he has prepared.

'If reality is what is real. What is real then?' asks Robert. 'Yes Kenny.'

'Matter and energy make up what is real as far as we know. That's what most scientists say.'

'Yes, Tom.'

(Applause for Kenny)

Tom is fair with fine, light coloured hair. He has a flat button nose and is wearing jeans and a white shirt.

'We know that the world is made up of atoms and electrons and particles,' he says. 'We can get a good idea of how the world is through science.'

'You're talking about matter,' says Robert. 'But scientists and physicists all say that they don't know the nature of matter. They keep looking for and finding, smaller and smaller particles that they think might be the basic building block of matter. It's like a scientific meatball where you just keep cutting it in half. Even if they thought they had found the smallest particle could they be sure that it was the smallest?'

(Applause for Tom)

Robert walks back along the side of the left hand block of seats and on to the stage. He stands in front of the lectern.

'So what is reality? What is real?' he asks.

'Our memories,' says George.

It is the first time George has shared. He has dark hair, a beard and spectacles. He is wearing a stripped rugby shirt and jeans.

'Welcome to the programme,' says Robert.

(Nervous laughter)

'You've been hiding here and there for a day and a half. At last you've decided to share something.'

George's face reddens.

'Memories,' says Robert. 'Bertram Russell said that it is not inconceivable that we were created five minutes ago with all of our memories and experiences of our perceived life intact. If anyone can prove that it is not the case I'll levitate back on to the stage.'

(Laughter)

'Of course it must be pointed out that just because you can't prove it isn't the case so you can't prove that it is either.'

(Applause for George)

'What about our perception. Reality is everything that we perceive.'

63

It is a female voice. I can't see who it is as the voice comes from the back of the room.

(Applause)

'OK,' says Robert. 'We're getting close to it now. Perception.'

Robert leans on the lectern.

'To identify what is real, first we need to understand how we perceive the world. Anyone got any ideas about how we perceive the world?'

'We see it, like Ray said,' says Cath.

(Applause)

'Just see?' asks Robert.

'Through all of our senses,' someone says.

(Applause)

'Which are?' Robert asks.

'Sight, hearing, touch, smell, taste,' says Karen.

(Applause)

'Yes! We perceive the world around us through our senses. We are constantly receiving information: sights, sounds, tastes, sensations and smells. Incidentally, by the time we have received this information through our senses, assimilated it and deciphered it with our brains, the event we have just witnessed has passed. We really experience the world in the past. All of the time.'

Robert moves from the stage and, once again, strolls towards the aisle between the two blocks of seats. It is as if he is doing a circuit of the room.

'We have a constant flow of information. We are bombarded with it. So! How do we know that the information that we are receiving is reality, is real, or is truthful? How do we know what's real?' Robert continues.

'When everybody agrees that the information is the same,' says Brian.

'Just because everyone agrees with something doesn't make it true. Everyone thought that the Earth was flat. It didn't make it true though.'

(Applause for Brian)

'How do we know that the information we are receiving is correct? How do we know if it is truthful? How do we know if things are really happening? How do we know that the world is really the way that we think it is? Can our senses deceive us?'

'Of course they can,' says Laura.

'In which way?' asks Robert. 'Give me an example.'

'Well the other week I was looking out of my window, it was twilight and it was getting dark. I could have sworn I saw an animal in my back yard.'

Laura has hennaed hair and pale skin with freckles. She is squinting like you would if you had forgotten your spectacles.

'Every time I looked out I could see its eyes, bright, like they were reflecting the light. As it got darker it was still there so I decided to investigate. It had been so still I thought it might be injured. Anyway when I went out and got closer I saw that it was in fact two pebbles that were lying together in such a way that, when they caught the light from the streetlight, they looked just like eyes.'

(Applause)

Various people share experiences in which their senses had played tricks on them. Someone recounts an experience with LSD. Another tells how they had mistaken somebody for someone else, when speaking to them on the phone, due to them expecting the caller to be the

65

other person.

'My boyfriend and I were always smelling tobacco in our flat and we don't smoke and neither did the people downstairs,' says Jaclyn.

Jaclyn is a bright bubbly lady with permed blonde hair.

'We joked that it was the ghost of a person that smoked but it turned out to be the chimney smelling when it got damp.'

(Applause)

'So what is the answer to the question? How do we know that the information we are receiving is correct? How do we know if things are really happening? How do we know that the world is really the way we think it is? How do we know what is real?'

Robert pauses for a few seconds.

'We don't,' says Tom. 'Intrinsically, as far as science is concerned, we don't.'

(Applause)

'So what *is* real then?' asks Carl.

Carl was sitting next to me the day before. I noticed that he had regularly dropped off to sleep during the proceedings. Carl appears like he's in his mid thirties. He has light brown hair that is over his ears but not down to his collar. He is wearing chino trousers and a long sleeve t-shirt with a waistcoat.

'What do *you* think is real,' Robert asks him.

'My job, my home, my family,' he says.

'Anyone seen Carl's Job?'

(Laughter)

'I didn't think so. Or his home or family? No! Look Carl. What we're saying is that you can't rely on the information that you receive through your senses. You can't prove what is real and what is not. Your job may look different to someone else, same as your family. To us, your home probably smells different than it does to you, How do you know what is real about it?'

'I know how I feel about them.'

'Bingo!' says Robert. 'YOU KNOW HOW YOU FEEL ABOUT THEM, YOUR EMOTION. WHAT YOUR EXPERIENCE OF THEM IS.'

Robert's voice becomes very loud and theatrical and then subsides to just, rather loud.

'That is, for us, the only realizable truth,' he continues. 'What experience we get about things. Yes Sarah.'

(Applause for Carl)

'I see it,' she says. 'You're saying that although we all agree how the world is, we all see it, or perceive it, differently due to a number of sensory factors.'

'And because of your beliefs,' Robert interjects. 'Go on,' he says.

'And because we see things differently and reality is not the same for everyone, the only thing that we can rely on is how we feel about something.'

'Yes Sarah. The only thing that we can rely on is: what our experience is about any given thing. What we *get*.'

(Applause for Sarah)

'And that's the funny thing,' Robert continues. 'The one thing, the only thing, that you can rely on to be true for you is the one thing that you avoid, the thing that you suppress: your experience. That's why so many of you walk around like constipated old ladies. Half the time you don't know what you are experiencing and the other half of the time, when you have an idea of what you're experiencing, you try and suppress it, avoid it. We've all seen it. Someone gets angry but they don't want to show or acknowledge it. You ask them, "You OK?" "I'm fine," they say and off they waddle with their buttocks firmly clenched, suppressing it. "Is everything OK?" "Can't complain," they say or some other platitude like, "mustn't grumble." And all the time they walk around with their sphincters shut like the aperture of a camera, and their buttocks clenched tight.'

Robert gives a masterful performance of someone walking with their buttocks clenched. It is uproariously funny, not least because most of us can identify with it. Robert walks up onto the stage still doing his impression of someone trying to hold a golf ball between their buttocks as they walk. People continue to laugh. He relaxes and stands in front of the lectern. It is not the first time that I am aware of Robert's exquisite timing and comic brilliance.

'You know how it is,' he continues. 'You walk into a party. What's the first thing you reach for? A cigarette? A drink? Any prop will do, anything to avoid the fact that you're frightened. Frightened of being on show, frightened of not being liked, whatever it is, there you are, frightened, shitting yourself.'

(Laughter)

'You desperately want to avoid your experience.'

Robert walks to the front of the stage and waits for the laughter to subside.

'We are unsure of what reality actually is. The information we receive through our senses is unreliable and our beliefs filter that information to make it even trickier,' he says.

'I still think that just because I believe something it doesn't necessarily have to get in the way of what I experience,' says Alan. 'Surely believing in something and experiencing it is the reasonable thing

68

to do.'

There are a few groans from the trainees. Again, some are weary of going over what they regard to be something we have already covered.

Alan is standing one row in front of where I am sitting. He is wearing dark brown cotton trousers and white tennis shoes. He has a t-shirt with an unbuttoned checked shirt over the top. I would guess he must be thirty years old. He has dark shoulder length hair. He looks like he just broke from rehearsing with his band.

'A reasonable thing to do,' repeats Robert. 'Oh that's reasonable alright.'

Robert moves quickly towards where Alan is standing. It is like he is in a hurry to get involved in an exchange.

'Reasonableness is the opposite of experience. You being reasonable, with your belief around whatever it may be, is a sure way to not experience what is really happening, a sure way to not be in touch with what is real. Well! I'm saying fuck your reasonableness Alan. Get in touch with what you are actually experiencing.'

'I'm sorry. I'm still not getting how belief gets in the way.'

'Alright,' says Robert. 'Let me ask you a question. When it comes to sex, do you like girls or do you prefer boys? Or maybe you're not fussy. You're OK with either.'

(Some laughter)

'No, I like girls,' says Alan.

He is smiling good-naturedly.

'Right,' says Robert. 'Let's imagine that you've met a nice looking girl and you're back at your place and you've had a nice evening and things have progressed and you start kissing. OK? Now you've got her down to her underwear and you're on top of her and you're starting with a bit of well practised foreplay.'

69

Robert is standing in the aisle between the two blocks of seats at the end of the row where Alan is standing.

'And you're being reasonable.'

(Some laughter)

'For fucks sake!' says Robert. 'You are being reasonable.'

(More laughter)

'You're wondering whether you, giving this lady your magic finger and tongue routine, will get her thinking how wonderful you are.'

(Even more laughter)

'Because you have a belief that when you make love to a woman she has to think that you are wonderful. Tell me Alan, with all his going on, are you in touch with your experience? Are you experiencing?'

'Probably not,' says Alan.

He is still smiling but blushing slightly.

'You're fucking right, probably not,' says Robert. 'So, back to the sex.'

Robert pokes his tongue out and makes a grotesque face whilst raising his arm in an obscene gesture.

(Huge laughter)

'You're happy that you've got her well and truly juiced up.'

(Laughter and some groans from a few of the female trainees)

'And you go for penetration. Now, you are of course concerned about whether or not the lady is going to have an orgasm. After all, no orgasm – no thinking how wonderful you are.'

(Laughter)

Alan is full on blushing now.

'So you're thinking that you're going to go for the reliable, slow, in out, technique from page 29 of the Kama Sutra guide to getting the girl to orgasm. This should get her off.'

70

(Laughter)

'While you're thinking all of this Alan. Are you experiencing?'

'No,' says Alan. 'But if it's really really nice for me, you know.'

I can see the back of Alan's neck and it is very red. Like he's sunburnt.

'I mean, if I'm not thinking about it I might be.'

'Of course you might be if you're not thinking. If you are not thinking, how can you be believing?' says Robert. 'And if you are not thinking and believing you are much more likely to be experiencing. OK.'

Robert nods his head at Alan. As Alan sits he turns around to look at the other trainees. He has a sheepish look on his face.

(Applause)

'Maybe that's why you arseholes like sex so much,' says Robert. 'It could well be the only time when you do, once in a while, switch off from thinking, suspend your beliefs and actually experience something. Maybe, for some of you, you switched off one time and really experienced and your sex lives are now just a search for that illusive moment. An attempt at recreating something you once *got*. Maybe that's why some of you are never satisfied with your sex lives. Why you're always trying new things, playing with new toys, changing partners.'

Robert returns to the low stage and stands by the lectern.

'OK,' he says. 'So, for us, the only reliable reality is our experience. Let's have a look at some of your experiences. Let's see if we can identify what your experience is, or was, in an event in your lives. It doesn't have to about sex, although with you lot it probably will be.'

(Nervous laughter)

'I want some sharing on things that have happened to you in your lives. Traumatic or trivial, it doesn't matter.'

71

People share some of their experiences, things that happened in their childhood or later in life. Astoundingly, with each person that shares, Robert identifies exactly their emotional experience and traces back to the underlying cause of that emotion. At times he drags it out, almost as if he is cross examining the sharer, almost like they have a reluctance to own up to something.

'Yes Miranda.'

Robert points to Miranda. She stands up. Miranda is tall and thin with straw coloured hair. She is wearing a long skirt with a blouse over a t-shirt. You might describe her as being willowy.

'I had a strange experience last week.'

She hesitates.

'And?' prompts Robert.

'When I was coming to the preview I saw someone who reminded me of my sister except it couldn't have been my sister. She was standing in the lobby of the hotel.'

'Why couldn't it have been your sister Miranda?'

'My sister died when I was ten.'

'How old was your sister?'

'She was younger than me, she was nearly eight. Anyway I felt like I wanted to go and tell her that she looked like my sister and I didn't. I felt sorry afterwards. I don't know why.'

Miranda goes to sit down but Robert tells her to wait. He moves towards her.

'Do you have any other brothers or sisters?'

'Yes a brother.'

'Is he older than you?'

'Two years older.'

'How did your sister die?' asks Robert.

'I didn't want to talk about that. I just wanted to share about the feeling I got when I saw the girl that looked like my sister.'

'And what was that feeling?'

'Like I said, I was sorry that I didn't say something to her.'

'How old was the girl who looked like your sister?'

'She looked eight!'

Strangely, Miranda's tone of voice is one that assumes everyone would know that.

'Was she on her own?'

'Yes,' says Miranda. 'She was standing in the lobby on her own, like she was waiting for someone.'

'What was your experience?'

'I felt sad that I didn't say anything to her.'

'What was your experience at the time you first saw the child?'

'I took a double look, I was shocked at first.'

'Shock is not an emotion it is a response. What did you feel?'

'Surprise.'

'Same with surprise.'

Robert goes on to the stage, to the white paper flip chart that stands on an easel to the right of the lectern.

'Wait there,' he says to Miranda.

Miranda remains standing.

'It is time we identified what our experience is,' says Robert. 'So that we can do this easily we are going to concentrate on the base emotions.'

He writes from the bottom of the paper in ascending order:

Apathy

Grief

Fear

Anger

Pride

Joy

'These are the base emotions. Most emotions can be traced back to these. We use these for expediency, to make it easier for us to identify our experience. There are a couple more that you will become aware of but we'll add those to the list later.'

A couple of hands go up. Miranda is still standing.

'We'll deal with Miranda's experience first then you can ask questions or have your say.'

Robert steps off the stage and walks back towards Miranda.

'Which one of those emotions did you get when you first saw the child?'

'Joy,' she says. 'For an instant, it was like I was pleased to see her but then I realized, of course, that it wasn't her.'

'And afterwards you were sad, your experience was grief.'

'Yes.'

'But it wasn't grief because you didn't say anything was it?'

'Yes.'

'No it wasn't, was it Miranda?'

Robert presses her and Miranda appears irritated when she replies.

'Yes of course it was. Why else.'

'How did your sister die Miranda?'

'In the pond, in the garden, she drowned.'

Tears start to run down Miranda's face. The room is silent except for the sound of Miranda sniffing. She wipes her cheeks with her sleeve. Tension sits in the room like a thick mist.

'What was her name?' Robert asks in soft voice.

'Emily.'

Miranda sniffs but makes no attempt to wipe her tears away as they continue to trickle down her face.

'Go back to that time,' says Robert. 'Where are you?'

The room is still silent. The trainees are fixated. I notice that a few others have tears in their eyes as well.

'In the garden.'

'Is it just the two of you?'

'Yes, my brother is away. I should be looking after her. We're playing hide and seek. I am hiding from her. She doesn't come so I go in the house. She still doesn't come so I go to look for her. Mummy is calling my name so I run to her. Daddy is in the pond, he is bringing her out.'

Now the tears are streaming down Miranda's face and she is sobbing deep sobs.

'You saw the child in the lobby and you experienced joy.'

Robert is speaking in a soft but clear voice.

'Then you remembered your grief at the time of that tragic event. What came after the grief Miranda?'

'I was annoyed with myself for letting everyone down. My sister, my parents. I should have been looking after her.'

Miranda starts to wipe away the tears again with her sleeve. She looks down at the black of her mascara that has stained her sleeve and lets out a little laugh.

'I've been carrying around that anger for the last sixteen years and I didn't even know I was angry,' she says.

'But you're not only angry with yourself are you?'

75

'No,' she says. 'My parents shouldn't have left me to look after her.'

'You were ten years old?'

'Yes.'

'And you have been angry with yourself and your parents because of this.'

'And my brother for not being there.'

Miranda is still smiling and wiping her face.

'How angry?'

'Fucking pissed off.'

Miranda laughs.

'Really fucking angry.'

Miranda sighs.

'I'm OK now. I loved my sister,' she says.

'Thank you,' says Robert.

Miranda sits and there is long and loud applause. People are wiping tears from their faces with their hands and sleeves and clapping at the same time. As the acknowledgement subsides hands go up.

'I just want to share that that was amazing,' says Tania.

Tania is still stroking her tears away.

'What was your experience,' Robert asks her. 'What did you get?'

'Grief, then joy,' she says.

'Thank you Tania.'

(Applause)

'Celia.'

'Yes, that was incredible. I didn't know until recently, that I had a younger sister who died at birth. I was angry that my parents hadn't told me but then I understood that they were trying to protect me. I really emphasised with Miranda.'

(Applause)

'Yes Jeff.'

Jeff is around thirty. He has black curly hair and a curly beard. He is wearing jeans and a t-shirt. Tufts of hair from his back and chest can be seen poking up at the top of his t-shirt.

'Can you run through the emotions that you have put up on the board?'

'No,' says Robert.

'But it will help us understand what's going on.'

'What! So you can run them through your belief system and compartmentalise and categorize them into your own comfy little racket?'

'No! We're supposed to be here to learn something. Surely having it explained will help.'

'No it won't help Jeff. I want you to all identify what your experience is and experience it. Get it?'

Jeff is shifting about uncomfortably on his feet.

'Well no,' he says.

'Keep your foot in the room and you will,' says Robert.

(Applause for Jeff)

'I'd like to share that I have been having trouble with the people who live in the flat downstairs and I am very frustrated when they don't listen to what I am concerned about,' says Lynne.

Lynne is probably in her late thirties. Her hair looks like it had been cut into a bob but has grown out. It gives her the appearance of a pageboy. The look is emphasised by the frilly collared white shirt that she wears under a purple waistcoat-like top.

'What trouble are you having?' asks Robert.

'Well, they often go outside late at night to smoke. They are renting the flat and I assume it is a no smoking flat. There is a security light that goes on and disturbs me. I like to sleep with the curtains not drawn on that window so I can enjoy the view when I wake up. I have spoken to them about it and they say they will be more careful but they are still doing it. I wanted to ask if the frustration I feel is anger.'

'Why don't you just close the curtain?'

'Because I would miss the view.'

'You could get the view when you are opening the curtains in the morning.'

'Well I could but I don't see why I should. Anyway, I am trying to identify what I experience.'

'Do you like to create drama in your life?' Robert asks.

Lynne looks shocked.

'No, of course not.'

'Then why are you standing up here telling us that you're inconvenienced about something no one in their right mind would care about or even give a thought to?'

'You asked us to try and identify what our experience was in a particular situation.'

Lynne shakes her head slightly as she speaks.

'You're so gummed up in your beliefs around the people downstairs and people in general that you can't possibly identify what your experience is. The consequence is that you can't experience what it is like to live, so you create a drama to try and re-create a feeling that you might have once had. Any feeling so long as it's a feeling. But when one pops up you repress that and you go back to creating another drama.'

Lynne's head shaking has increased. She is moving her head from side to side with her mouth open.

'Get off of it for fuck's sake Lynne. Don't wallow in the drama.

Start to live a little. Join them downstairs for a cigarette, better still, take a joint down.'

(Some laughter)

'Or tell them how you really feel. How do you feel now?'

'I'm upset.'

Lynne's bottom lip is starting to wobble.

'Grief Lynne. You are *getting* grief.'

'I've never been spoken to like that before.'

'You've got your bit of drama now Lynne but this time you know what you are experiencing.'

'Yes, grief.'

Lynne is sobbing.

'Go with it. Try and identify the physical characteristics of the experience. What does the grief feel like? What colour is it? Is it heavy or light? Explore it. Be with it. Thank you Lynne.'

(Applause)

There is more sharing in which people recount things that have happened to them and the associated emotional experience. Some are harrowing like Miranda's, some appear to me to be more trivial.

'Yes?'

It is Jeff again.

'I want to say that I am angry with being blanked in that way earlier.'

'Good,' says Robert. 'How angry?'

'Fucking angry as a matter of fact. We are in an untenable position down here. We can only speak when we're picked and we can't say anything if we're cut off.'

79

'So, the drama is that you are peeved because you didn't get your way.'

(Laughter)

'So, what is your experience? What is the reality for you?'

'That I'm fucking angry.'

'Experience it, don't try and change it. Where in your body is the anger?'

'In my chest.'

'What does it feel like?'

'A ball. Like a clenched fist.'

'How deep in your chest?'

'About here,' says Jeff.

He looks down, points to a spot in the middle of his chest and then laughs.

'It's gone now.'

Jeff goes to sit but Robert stops him.

'Hang on,' he says. 'What are you getting now?'

Jeff looks up at the board.

'Pride,' he says. 'Normally I lose my temper quite easily and I don't like it. This time I controlled it.'

'No! You didn't control it. You experienced it and it transformed itself. Thank you Jeff.'

(Applause)

As we acknowledge Jeff's sharing someone stands and hurries towards the back of the room, towards the door. It is Martin, the man who has the crust around his eyes and the odd stare. He is stopped by two trainers at the back. The trainees turn to watch the commotion. The trainers restrain him but Martin struggles to free himself and kicks out and tries to wrestle himself loose. Two more trainers help to subdue him.

Finally he calms down. Robert arrives at the back and speaks to Martin in an almost hypnotic voice. He tells him to relax. He tells him that he can leave but they can't let him storm out and go running under a bus. Eventually Martin is led out. The trainers return to their seats, seemingly unfazed and with the same neutral expressions. Robert returns to the front.

'We'll give him a little while to calm down and then get him home,' he says.

The excitement has the effect of subduing the room.

'Phew!' says Greg. 'Thah thah that wuh wuh wuh was heavy.'

'What did you get from that,' asks Robert.

'Fuh Fuh Fear,' stutters Greg. 'Uh Uh I hate cah cah confrontation.'

Robert goes into the nature of Greg's experience surrounding confrontation. It seems Greg's dislike of confrontation may have come from when his parents lived with his grandparents. Greg remembered his mother arguing with his grandmother almost every day. He says that he remembers feeling the tension in the house. He says he remembered the relief when they moved out of his grandparents' house and into their own home.

'Th the tuh tensions returned wuh when muh my grandparents came to visit though,' he says.

Roberts draws out from Greg that his grandparents never thought that his mother was good enough for his father: their son.

'Thah thah that's why I I gah gah get fuh fuh fear.'

Greg says that his fear is fear of people not being liked or accepted.

'Ah ah of muh me noh noh not buh being liked.'

The trainees acknowledge Greg. I am sure that his stutter is getting less severe. I wonder if it is because he is more accustomed to everyone and feels more confident. I wonder if his stutter started at the time when there were problems with his grandparents and mother.

The sharing goes on.

At any one time about a quarter of the trainees switch off. We go from being tired to feeling irritated at what someone is sharing, just as we did in the last session. Our backsides ache again, as do our backs. Some are busting for that cigarette, some, like me, are trying to ignore their grumbling empty stomachs and I'm sure there are a few wanting to get to the lavatory again. We have little idea of the time except that this seems like it has been going on for hours. Robert is still fresh. He still looks exactly the same as he did when he first entered the room, as do the trainers.

'Don't their faces ache from keeping those blank expressions,' whispers Ray.

Ray is sitting next to me.

'Got something to share Ray?' asks Robert.

Ray is caught. He shakes his head.

'If you've got something to share, you know the procedure.'

'I was just joking about the trainers and wondering how they managed to keep the same expressions,' he says.

'It's easy,' says Robert. 'They've stopped being arseholes. Why don't you try it?'

Everyone, including Ray, laughs.

It's strange but when there is laughter the mood in the room seems to lighten, people wake up, our backsides don't seem to ache as much. The relief is short lived though. All of the negative feelings soon return as the sharing continues.

'I've never felt that I was any good at anything,' Miriam is saying.

She is a small woman who looks like a little bird with her yellow cardigan and long thin nose.

'I'd really like to be good at something.'

'Why don't you think you are good at anything Miriam?' Robert asks.

'I don't know,' she says.

Miriam has a high voice. It has a sort of sing – song quality to it.

'How do you feel about not being good at anything?'

'Well kind of unhappy.'

'You mean that you experience grief?'

'Not really grief,' she says. 'More embarrassment when I'm asked to do something and I can't get it right.'

'What is it you do Miriam?'

'I am studying to be an actress. I really want to be good at it but it just won't come.'

'So you're saying you're not a good actress?'

'Yes, sort of.'

'You're making a pretty good job of it now.'

(Laughter)

'Why don't you try getting off of your *little girl lost* racket and start to experience life. You might find out that you are a better actress than you give yourself credit for.'

Miriam turns her head and makes an expression that resembles shock and surprise.

83

'I don't know what you mean.'

'I mean that you can't go on being Daddy's little girl all your life.'

Miriam interrupts, 'I'm very close to my father. He has always supported me no matter what.'

Her voice has gone down half an octave and she is red in the face.

'Even though he doesn't want you to be actress he still supports you.'

'Yes,' she says.'

Once again, I am aware of the ability Robert has of getting to the crux of what the person's sharing is actually about.

'He wanted me to work with him and mother but I was determined to study acting.'

'And you wound him round your finger with your *Daddy's little girl* racket. So what?'

Miriam is red in the face. She wipes away a tear.

'When I'm working I feel I can't let them down. My parents, they've given up a lot to send me to drama school. That's why I get embarrassed when I make a mistake.'

'Embarrassment is a secondary emotion,' says Robert. 'Embarrassment is really anger. What are you angry about?'

'I'm angry that I can't do it,' she spurts out.

'Are you worried that you'll disappoint them?'

'Yes. I start off angry then I'm frightened that I will let them down'

'Yes,' says Robert. 'But when you avoid your experience of anger the anger can transform itself into another emotion. A more base emotion. It's the next one down the scale,' he says.

84

Robert points to the white flip board.

'If you truly experience your anger and get in touch with it, you will find that it disappears or transforms itself in a positive direction. When you suppress or avoid your experience you can end up all the way down the scale to apathy. Thank you Miriam.'

(Applause)

'What do we need to do to transform these emotions?' asks Carol.

Carol seems to have overcome her initial timidity.

'We'll be covering that in some detail later,' says Robert. 'For now I want you to share your experiences and tell us what you got.'

Robert turns and walks down the aisle between the two blocks of seats.

'There are still some of you who are not sharing. It's no good thinking you can hide as if you were behind a curtain. Don't forget, I can see your toes poking out underneath. Don't make me start picking you.'

And the sharing goes on. We continue to acknowledge the person sharing with applause. Sometimes the applause is muted and Robert reminds us to acknowledge the person who has shared, more enthusiastically. This draws my attention to the fact that my hands are getting sore as well as my backside.

Occasionally someone shares something completely unrelated to the discussion. Cleverly, Robert always brings the subject back to where he wants it to be.

'I just want to share that I don't think some people are being totally honest about their experience.'

It is Laura. She is wearing spectacles now.

'Be specific,' says Robert.

'Pat said earlier that when he finished his studies and got his degree he got joy but that is not what I got. I thought he was having a bit of an ego trip.'

'You spotted that did you?' asks Robert.

'Yes.'

'That's because it is Pat's racket. That is how he wants everyone to see him: As the earnest truth seeker striding towards enlightenment and ready to pass that on through his teaching.'

Robert smiles wryly.

'I didn't point it out because I know that he will get off that racket before the end of the seminar.'

Laura sits down.

'Don't sit Laura,' he says. 'What about you? Did you go to university?'

'No I did not,' she says firmly.

'Not bright enough?'

Robert raises his eyebrows.

(Some laughter)

'My family concentrated on getting my older brother through. We didn't have much money.'

'You sacrificed your own education to help him?'

'In a way, yes.'

'How do you feel about that?'

'I am happy at having helped him and my family.'

'What crap!' says Robert.

Laura looks stunned.

'Maybe it is true. You just weren't bright enough.'

'I am just as bright as him but he's the son.'

'What do you get Laura? When you think about your brother going to University and graduating and then coming home and being slapped on the back and congratulated?'

'Well, I suppose I am a little jealous. I might have been cross that I didn't have the chance.'

'Cross!' Robert says through a laugh. 'Pah! You are angry. You are right royally pissed off, fuming angry. How dare they lavish all of that on *him*, just because he's the boy?'

'Well yes, I am angry about it.'

'But you're not going to say anything to them, are you. You're not going to say, "It's unfair," or, "Fuck you, I'm going to University anyway," are you? You're just going to keep your racket going, your racket of *poor, hard done by, me*. And then to cap it off you're going to transfer your shit onto Pat over there because he is a smug fucker like your brother.'

Laura stands open mouthed. I would love to see what Pat looks like but I can't pick out where he is sitting.

'We've all got rackets that we cling to Laura. The drama is that your parents gave your brother more of an opportunity to go to university. The reality is, your experience is......'

Robert waits. Once again he raises his eyebrows. He has a 'Well?' expression on his face.

'As I said I am cross.'

'You're not fucking cross are you Laura. Unclench your fucking buttocks for a moment.'

'I am very angry about it.'

'What do you get Laura?'

'Anger,' Laura says meekly.

'Shout it out Laura. Be angry. Get in touch with it. SHOUT IT!'

'I AM BLOODY ANGRY,' shouts Laura.

'Come on. Shout it out again.'

'I AM FUCKING BLOODY ANGRY.'

Laura is red in the face, as red as her hair.

'I AM FUCKING BLOODY ANGRY,' she shouts again.

'Thank you Laura.'

(Applause)

After a couple of minutes Laura raises her hand again.

'I just want to say that I apologise to Pat.'

'No need to clamber back on to your racket Laura,' says Robert.

(Applause)

The sharing continues for what seems like, and must be, hours. We trainees share our stories and gradually identify what our experience is. The session is long and I find myself really struggling to stay with it, to stay awake. Really it is only the ache in my back and the pain of my sore buttocks that keep me from falling asleep.

Finally, Robert tells us that we can have a break for an hour and a half. I collect my watch. It is eight o'clock in the evening. Once again the routines of lavatory, smoke and eat are carried out. I struggle to a restaurant around the corner. I am with Snick, Marjory and Carol. Although my back is sore and my legs are stiff from sitting, the relief of being off my backside makes up for it. I almost wish I could eat standing up.

'I wonder what will happen to Martin,' says Carol.

'Ask Robert,' says Snick.

'Do you reckon he'll get his money back?' I ask.

'It was weird, him freaking out like that, I mean,' Snick continues. 'Must have got too much for him. Maybe he's claustrophobic or something.'

'He looked a bit odd. Did you notice his eyes?' I ask.

'He looked like he had conjunctivitis,' says Carol.

We are back in the room with our name tags on and our watches and paraphernalia removed. We are seated and waiting. The trainers are in their positions with their neutral expressions. A good number of the trainees already look like they are having difficulty staying awake. I suppose it is the exertion of the training followed by dinner. Robert enters the room and walks along the side, in front of where the trainers are seated. He invites more sharing on our experiences which goes on for what seems like more than an hour. There is, however, a slight difference in Roberts' dynamic. He has started to emphasise a separation between the event and the experience. He is directing the sharers to focus on their emotional experience.

'I was thinking about what Laura said earlier. I was born in August so when I started school I was four years and one month old, nearly a year younger than some of the other kids. I was put in the lower stream. The stream that was less academic,' says John. 'I sort of gave up and messed around in school and never tried.'

John is in his late twenties. He is around six feet tall. He is wearing jeans and a blue shirt.

'I regret it now but I also feel that I never got a chance.'

'So that's the drama,' says Robert. 'What is the reality? What is your experience?'

'It started out that I thought I was experiencing grief but now I

89

feel that I'm angry about it, angry with the school and with myself.'

'You're fucking angry now,' says Robert.

'Yes I am,' says John starting to smile.

'Did you notice that your first experience was grief but when you acknowledged your experience it transformed to anger?'

'Yes I did.'

'And what do you get now?'

'Nothing,' says John.

He is smiling.

'Actually, I feel great,' he says.

(Applause)

'I was out with a friend the other week and we took a wrong turning and found ourselves walking past a pub full of blokes. They were spilling out onto the pavement, all blokes. Some whistled, a couple shouted. My friend wasn't worried at all. She thought it was a laugh but I was frightened. It reminded me a bit of when the ol' man used to come in drunk and fool around with my mum it always used to end up in a row. I suppose that's why I was frightened,' says Kay.

Kay is pretty and a little plump in a pleasant way. She has very blue eyes and a South London accent.

'So walking past these drunken men and having the memory of your father's drunken behaviour is the drama. So what is the reality?'

'I experienced fear.'

Robert nods his head. Kay sits.

(Applause)

Throughout this period of sharing Robert continues to emphasise the difference between the event perceived through our senses and our experience. The sharing of experiences goes on. There is, however, very little input from people not sharing. It is unsurprising as it is after our dinner break I, for one, find that I am stifling yawns and struggling to stay awake. I see others are the same or at the very least having difficulty concentrating.

'The energy levels in this room are really low and dropping,' declares Robert.

He is right. The sharing and the response to the sharing, has become rather sluggish.

'We are going to finish with a couple of processes. The first is a process to get the energy back into the room,' he says.

We are called up in groups of around twenty and directed to a section of wall which we are told to push against as hard as we can. The trainers move from their seated positions and assist us by directing the placement of our hands and shoulders. Their expressions are neutral, as they have been for the two days of the seminar so far.

Robert encourages us by saying things like, 'Come on, get your back into it,' and, 'Push!' Harder! Let's push that wall down.'

Tired but re-energised we return to our seats and watch the next batch take over. I estimate that the process takes almost an hour.

There is a brief period of sharing about the pushing process. Once again Robert concentrates on what we *got*.

'Yeh! I really gave it a good shove,' says Sarah.

'What was your experience? What did you get?'

'I was pleased with myself for really pushing.'

(Applause)

Robert says that there is one final thing that we are going to do before we are allowed out. It is a relaxation process. We are directed to find a space on the floor, behind the two blocks of chairs, in which to lie down on. We are told to make ourselves as comfortable as possible and to have our eyes closed.

'I want you to concentrate on your big toe on your left foot.'

Robert's voice is quieter and softer.

'When you have located the toe I want you to envisage it. Concentrate on its form, its contours, its temperature, its weight. Now relax it. Focus on relaxing the toe. Now go on to the whole foot. Create a picture of it in your mind. Let the whole foot relax. Let it sink into the floor as if the floor was a soft mattress.'

Robert waits, perhaps thirty seconds.

'Now focus on your right foot.'

He directs us to undertake the same procedure. After another thirty seconds, he continues.

'Now concentrate on your left calf.'

Once again we go through the same procedure. After the calf we move on to the thighs. Left then right. Then onto the torso.

'Relax the area in and around your stomach. Let its weight drop through your back and sink into the floor.'

We go onto the chest, shoulders and then the arms. I find myself in a blissfully relaxed state. Every part of my body feels like it is floating, suspended in the air.

'Imagine yourself to be weightless, floating. From your shoulders move to your head. Relax the chin. Feel its weight, let it rest.'

We go on to the lips, the nose the cheeks, the forehead, the top of the head. The room is silent save for the sound of relaxed breathing.

'Now imagine a point six inches from the top of your head.'

Robert's voice is almost hypnotic.

'Relax that point. Imagine that there is a rod from that point attached to your head. With the point above your head acting as a fulcrum spin on its axis.'

Robert waits for a few minutes and then brings us round. People stretch and yawn as they return to their seats.

'There is on final thing,' says Robert. 'How many people here use an alarm clock to wake up?'

A couple of dozen hands go up.

'If I don't set my alarm I'd never wake up,' says Tania.

(Applause)

'I have to have one,' says Amanda. 'I always oversleep if I don't set my clock.'

(Applause)

'I have one as a back-up. I always wake up before it rings and turn it off,' says Brian.

(Applause)

'Just for once, as an experiment, I want you to programme yourselves to wake up tomorrow morning without an alarm clock,' says Robert. 'I want you to make a request of yourselves to wake up at a certain time.'

'How do we do that?' asks Sarah. 'And what if we're late? Will we get in trouble?'

'If you are late you will be in big trouble,' says Robert.

Robert pulls an angry, threatening face that is menacing yet at the same time hilariously funny.

(Laughter)

'Just try it,' he continues. 'Tell yourselves to wake up at a certain time. You might be surprised.'

'I'll request myself to wake up at seven but set my alarm for seven thirty just in case,' says Sarah.

(Applause)

Robert's idea of waking up without an alarm is interesting for me as I always do wake up without an alarm. It is only now that I am conscious of saying to myself, 'Up at seven,' or whatever, before I go to sleep.

The day concludes with Robert sorting out the logistics of lifts and getting everyone to where they are going. We retrieve our watches and paraphernalia and leave. It is one thirty in the morning. I give lifts to Jed and Marjory and Tania and Sarah. The two girls have arranged to stay the night with Marjory so as to make it easier for them to get in on the Sunday.

First Sunday

I am surprised at the fact that I am not tired. Getting four and a half hours sleep after a long and gruelling day would normally leave me feeling jaded. Today though, I have a spring in my step as I hurry past the last minute smokers and enter the hotel. I am with Jed, Marjory, Tania and Sarah. I had agreed to pick them up as I had done the previous day.

We are seated in the room as before. We have handed in our watches and bags and coats. We are wearing our name badges. The trainers are seated in the same places with the same stony expressions. Today, when Robert enters the room and walks along the side, in front of the trainers, and says, 'Good morning,' the response is noticeably more energised.

We start with some sharing about the previous day. People tell how relaxed they were during and after the final process.

'I had the best night's sleep I've had for years,' says Brian. 'I got home and slept like a log. My wife, who's already done the seminar, said that I had a smile on my face as I slept. She said I still snored though.'

(Laughter and applause)

'I didn't get much sleep but I feel I didn't need it. We were up half the night talking,' says Sarah, nodding in Tania's direction. 'I had no problem getting up without my alarm clock. I went to sleep at three and woke up at seven like I had ordered myself.'

(Applause)

'It was very interesting,' says James. 'I charged myself to wake at six thirty and I did. Normally, when I am short of sleep, as I have been these last few days, I struggle to wake without an alarm. This morning I had no problem. I even left my wife sleeping. I didn't have to disturb her.'

(Applause)

'I think I might be starting to enjoy the seminar,' says Karen.

'Don't worry,' says Robert. 'We'll soon put a stop to that.'

(Laughter, then applause for Karen)

'Can I just ask? What happened to Martin?' It is Tania.

'We calmed him down and he went home. He is fine. He has chosen to complete the seminar and will be attending the next one.'

(Applause)

I am impressed that Tania cared enough to ask. I get the feeling the others were too. It is clear they are happy that the Martin issue has been resolved to some degree of satisfaction. There appears to be a comradeship forming amongst the trainees, a sort of blitz spirit, a sense that we are all in this together.

'Did everybody *get it* regarding beliefs and experience,' asks Robert.

'I got that our beliefs get in the way of us understanding our experience,' says Chas.

I hadn't noticed Chas before. He is small and dark with a cheery face. He is wearing a capped sleeved t-shirt on top of a long sleeved one.

'Don't try and understand what experience you're getting. Experience it. Get in touch with it.'

'I would also like to share that when I got home last night my flatmates were smoking joints but I didn't join in. I was very proud of myself for keeping my agreement.'

96

Robert walks to the side, where Chas is standing.

'What is your belief around the criminalisation of cannabis use?' he asks.

'I believe that it's wrong. It should be legal,' says Chas. 'And not just because I like a puff.'

'And what's your experience around it?'

'Anger,' says Chas. 'I get angry because it's less harmful than tobacco or alcohol.'

'Is it always anger?' asks Robert.

'Unless I'm stoned,' says Chas.

(Laughter)

'Then I don't care.'

(More laughter)

'Getting stoned is a first class way of avoiding your experience,' says Robert. 'How do you feel not having any dope?'

'Funnily enough, I feel really good,' says Chas beaming.

(Applause)

The sharing continues for another half an hour or so. People stand and share things like, how they felt about the previous day's proceedings, what they *got* from it, their opinion of what the last person said and so on.

Robert is on the stage standing next to the lectern.

'We've seen that we receive information through our senses. This information is filtered through our beliefs and we *get* our experience. We have seen that if you get in touch with, explore, understand and fully experience what you *get* then the experience can be transformed.'

Robert looks around at the trainees as if he is checking that he has everyone's attention.

'This is because of one of the irrefutable truths of the universe. Namely that *change causes persistence and persistence causes change.*'

Robert waits for a few seconds as if he is gauging our reaction.

'When we try and change something it persists but when we don't try and change it, when we just observe it and experience it, there is a transformation, a change.'

Robert turns a leaf over on the white paper flip chart pad and writes the words: *change causes persistence and persistence causes change.*

'Who noticed, yesterday, that when they didn't try and change their experience, it disappeared?'

'I noticed.'

It is Miranda whose sister had drowned.

'I discovered that I was angry with myself, my parents and my brother but then I identified it. I just went with the experience. I felt the anger like a wave coming over me, like water filling my nose and mouth, like drowning, like my sister. Then it subsided and seemed to fade away. I was left with nothing. Peace.'

(Applause)

Robert nods his head in an understanding gesture.

'You acknowledged your experience without trying to change it and it transformed into something else.'

'When I was listening to Miranda's story I was aware that I was experiencing grief,' says Carol. 'But I just let it go. It then became happiness after Miranda had acknowledged her experience. I'm also not frightened anymore about getting up and speaking. Everyone here has helped me with that too.'

Carol blushes slightly and makes a little hand waive gesture

98

before sitting.

(Applause)

'I didn't have the slightest clue of what's going on and I still don't,' says Matt.

Matt is young, in his early twenties. He has a slightly unkempt look, like he just got out of bed.

'All this stuff about believing and experiencing, it goes straight over my head. Everyone is getting up and sharing stuff that I don't want to hear. I'm not saying it's bollocks or anything, it's just that it's like, intimate. You know what I mean. Can't you just tell us what we've got to do then we can all go home.'

(Laughter)

'How do you feel when people are up sharing,' asks Robert.

'With some I switch off. I mean, I don't give a fuck about their trivial problems. There's far greater problems in the world other than, I was sad 'cos my pet rabbit died.'

(Laughter)

'The others? I just wish they'd shut the fuck up.'

'So with some you get apathy, you can't be bothered, and others piss you off, you get angry.'

'Yeh!' Says Matt.

He is smiling like he's enjoying having the spotlight on him.

'So whatever the underlying reasons are for you getting apathetic or angry, they are the drama of the situation. They are judgements based on acquired beliefs from information that comes through your senses. You with me?'

'Yeh!' says Matt

He nods his head in agreement.

'We have shown that this information is inherently unreliable in terms of what is real. OK'

Matt nods again.

'And we've identified that the only thing that we can rely on is what we get, our experience.'

'Yes.'

'In your case your experience is apathy and anger. Got it?'

Matt continues nodding.

'Now I am letting you in on a little secret. And that is, that change causes persistence and persistence causes change. If you give up trying to avoid your experience, trying to change your experience, of apathy or anger in your case, and you get in touch with it and experience it, then it will transform itself.'

Robert has walked towards Matt and is standing at the end of the row where Matt is standing.

'What were your stated aims? What did you want to get out of this seminar?'

'I'm unemployed at the moment and can't decide what I want to do. I thought this might help.'

Matt shuffles his feet. He looks less happy at being in the spotlight now.

'The reason that you can't decide what to do, and ultimately have ended up doing fuck all, is because you have been avoiding your experience. Whatever your experience is, you avoid it. Because of that, the experience persists. So you come on this programme, angry and apathetic, and tell us how shit or insignificant you believe everyone else is. Well that's fine Matt but by the end of the seminar whether you understand it or not you will *get it*. You will acknowledge your experience and not try and change it. Maybe then you'll see that perhaps not everybody other than you is insignificant or shit.'

The trainees applaud loudly. I suspect that the enthusiasm is not so much acknowledgement for Matt but more approval of Robert's response.

'Mind you,' says Robert as he returns to the front. 'Maybe it will turn out that we all *are* insignificant and shit apart from Matt.'

(Laughter)

'I just want to share that I think Matt's problems are insignificant and shit,' Says Andrea.

Andrea is a girl with a Mediterranean skin. She is in her early twenties and is wearing a gypsy like headscarf.

(Laughter and applause)

As before, the sharing goes on. The emphasis of Robert's responses is on the premise that change causes persistence and persistence causes change. As the trainees share, Robert continues to point out how, by avoiding, suppressing and trying to change ones experience, those experiences persist and that, in many cases, it is this persistence of the same experiences that, he says, stop our lives from working.

'We saw it yesterday,' Robert is saying. 'Those of you who shared an experience, when you went with it and observed it and got in touch with the physical sensations of it, it disappeared. It is the resistance that causes the experience to persist.'

'I've read, though, that it is often best to not think about negative emotions, that negativity can make you ill,' says James. 'Surely that's preferable to facing things head on or confronting it as you call it.'

'I don't know where you read that James but I can inform you that.'

101

Robert walks towards where James is standing. He voice is gentle and carries a tone like he is agreeing with James.

'IT IS COMPLETE AND UTTER BOLLOCKS.'

Robert changes his tone and speaks the last sentence in a loud voice. The contrast gives a dramatic effect.

'Resistance is the best way to make yourself ill,' he continues. 'Imagine going around bottling things up all of your life. You're going to be like a pressure cooker. You'll let a bit of steam off with a couple of drinks or a joint but the pressure is still there. Got a headache? I'm not surprised with all that avoided experience. Take an aspirin. You may think you've got it under control by using your little helpers to keep the lid on but one day, one day.'

Robert repeats the last two words and shakes his head.

'Think about it,' he continues. 'The Chinese call it yin and yang. If you have someone pushing and you push back what's going to happen. You're going to be pushing forever. Opposites cancel each other out. For all you scientists out there. Absolute zero, minus two hundred and seventy three point one five degrees centigrade. Nought degrees Kelvin. It's the temperature at which all fundamental particles of nature cease to vibrate. They stop moving, stop changing. And what happens? Disintegration. Non persistence. Change cause persistence and persistence causes change.'

(Applause for James)

'Yesterday, when I got in touch with my grief, I stopped trying to change it and it went,' says Caroline.

I would guess that Caroline is in her mid forties. She is tall and slender. She is wearing a plum coloured cardigan over a cream blouse and blue jeans which are pressed and have a crease in them.

'When I got home I spoke to my friend about it and he said it

102

could have been because I'd spoken about in public. That it had a cleansing effect.'

'It was because you gave up wanting to change it,' says Robert.

'But it could be both couldn't it?' Caroline continues.

'Sharing it or saying it out loud can add weight to your not trying to change it. It can help you focus on the elements of your experience, help you get in touch with it.'

Robert is looking quizzically at Caroline.

'Has your friend done the seminar?' he asks.

'No but he is a psychologist. He recommended that I take the seminar. It is because of him that I am here. I was looking at some courses to take that would help me with my writing. I'm starting out as a writer. He chose the seminar for me.'

'Are you in a relationship with him?'

'No,' says Caroline. 'He is only recently divorced.'

'Does he tell you what colour knickers to put on in the morning?' asks Robert.

There is laughter and some sniggering. Someone lets out a barely audible gasp of shock.

Carline is standing in the opposite block to where I am seated but close enough for me to see her eyes widen.

'I beg your pardon,' she says.

It is like she can't believe what Robert has asked her.

'I mean, do you do everything he says?' asks Robert.

'No.'

'Get off of your racket then, and take responsibility for your life. It was your choice to attend the seminar. Don't load up the responsibility for you being here onto the poor sod's shoulders,' says Robert. 'He's got enough to do picking out your pants.'

(Laughter)

'Well, there's no reason to be insulting about somebody you have not met.'

'I'm not insulting him. I am pointing out to you that it is your responsibility for being here, your choice. If you're going to stay in the room do so because it is your choice.'

Robert is standing at the side of the right hand block of seats. Close to where Caroline is standing.

'Do you get that?' he asks in a firm manner.

'I am here because he recommended I attend. I chose to accept his recommendation.'

'Whatever the circumstances, whatever the drama that led to you choosing to be here, do you accept that being here is your choice?'

'Well yes.'

Caroline says the words almost grudgingly.

'Thank you Caroline.'

(Applause)

'He probably recommended that you do the seminar because he was taking responsibility and trying to get you to unclench your buttocks and get in touch with your experience,' he adds.

(Some laughter)

'And right there is another reason why your lives don't work. You arseholes don't take responsibility for your actions.'

Robert pauses and looks out over the trainees. He is back up on the stage, standing next to the lectern.

'I had hoped that, by now, you might be starting to cotton on to what is going on,' he continues. 'Who creates your experience?'

He walks to the side of the stage.

'Come on. WAKE UP OUT THERE,' he shouts. 'Who creates

your experience?'

'We do?' asks Tania.

'We do,' says Robert. 'Damn right. We create our experience. And what is the only thing that we can take to be real, the only thing we can be sure of?'

'Our experience,' says Tania.

'We.'

Robert stabs his finger at his chest three or four times.

'We create our reality,' he says.

Robert is standing at the front of the stage. He is right on the edge.

'And we have to take responsibility for creating it.'

He walks along the edge and steps down.

'Acknowledge Tania,' he says.

(Applause)

'Nobody does anything that they don't want to do,' he continues.

He waits to see the reaction of the trainees.

'You, have to take responsibility for everything that happens,' he adds. 'Everyone get it? Everyone agree?'

'No,' says Amanda. 'I do plenty of things that I don't want to do,'

'Such as?' asks Robert.

'I don't want to go to work but I have to.'

'You don't *have* to go to work. You could stay at home.'

'But then I wouldn't have any money. How would I feed myself and pay my rent?'

'I can think of plenty of alternative options,' says Robert. 'You could live in a tent and grow your own food.'

'I'd still need money.'

'The fact of the matter is that you choose to go to work. It is your choice, your decision.'

'It isn't,' says Amanda. 'I have to go. I don't want to but I have to. Otherwise I won't have any money.'

'You don't *have* to,' says Robert. 'Like I say, live without money.'

'You can't live without money though.'

'You choose not to live without money, so you choose to go to work. Your choice. Thank you Amanda.'

(Applause)

'The fact is that going to work or not is Amanda's choice. She wants to go to work because she wants the money. Her choice. Yes Jed.'

'Yes but there's a difference between choosing to do something and wanting to do something.'

'Give me an example.'

'Well,' says Jed scratching his chin. 'I wanted to lie in bed this morning because I was really tired after yesterday but I chose to get up because a wanted to finish the seminar. Even though I didn't want to get up. In order to do what I wanted I had to get up.'

'You can't compartmentalise your acts. You either want to get up and finish the seminar or you want to stay in bed and not finish it. What did you choose?'

'To get up and finish it I suppose,' says Jed.

(Applause)

'I purposely used the phrase *Nobody does anything that they don't want to do*, to stimulate discussion. We could go on and argue about the semantics of words for the rest of the day. The fact of the matter is that we chose to do everything that we do, we want to do it and we

106

have to take responsibility for it. Yes Peter.'

Peter is around five feet eight tall and what you might call stout. He has a thick neck and a muscular frame.

'I've got chronic tinnitus,' he says. 'I was in the navy and I got tinnitus because of the loudness of the weapons fire. I didn't choose to get it.'

(Applause)

'Yes Snick.'

'I think I get it,' he says. 'Peter chose to join the navy where there was a good chance that there would be weapons fire. He didn't have to join up, he chose to. He didn't have to stand next to the guns. It might be a bit harsh but he has to take responsibility for his choices that led to him getting tinnitus.'

(Applause)

'That's rubbish,' says Richard.

Richard looks to be in his thirties. He is well spoken. He has short dark hair. He is just under six feet tall and wears Farah trousers and an open neck shirt with a stripped v-neck pullover. He looks like he's just left the bar at the golf club.

'My car got stolen two weeks ago. How is that my fault?'

'Where was it stolen from?'

'It was parked in town. I was shopping with my fiancé.'

'You bought the car didn't you?' says Robert.

'Yes.'

'You were aware that some cars that people buy occasionally get stolen?'

'Well yes but.'

'And you parked the car. You chose to leave it somewhere where it might get stolen?'

107

'I didn't know it would get stolen from where I parked it.'

'Lapse of you wasn't it. I mean, you not taking responsibility for finding out where the car theft hot spots in your neighbourhood are.'

(Laughter)

'How did you feel when your car was removed?'

'Very angry. We had to get a taxi home.'

(Laughter)

'Who created the experience of anger?'

'Well, I suppose I did.'

'You created the experience of being angry because you chose to perceive the car as being stolen. Had you perceived it as being borrowed you might have created a different experience. Look,' continues Robert. 'You have to take responsibility for being in the world. That means being aware that you create everything you experience. It doesn't mean you have to tell that to the Insurance Company.'

(Laughter)

'You have to take responsibility for the fact that they will do everything possible to not pay out on a claim.'

(More laughter)

'OK OK,' says Richard as he sits.

(Applause)

'You see, people are ingrained with a sense of non responsibility. It starts when you're very young. You see it all the time. Here's little Johnny, he's running around the living room and he bumps into a chair and bangs his knee. Up comes mummy and comforts him. "Naughty chair," she says. "Hurting Johnny like that," and she slaps the chair.'

(Laughter)

'Never mind naughty chair. It wasn't the fucking chair's fault.

108

The chair wasn't waiting to bump into little Johnny. It's a fucking inanimate object. Little Johnny needs to be more careful when he's running around like a maniac.'

(More laughter)

'Keep on like that and Johnny's going to be a victim all of his life.'

Robert is standing at the front of the stage.

'Oh why does it always have to happen to me?'

Robert acts out the lament of someone who feels that everything is against him.

'Why me? It's not my fault; I didn't do it.'

The intonation of Robert's speech and his actions are once again hilarious. There is much laughter from the trainees. When someone asks why the trainers don't appear to find it funny I turn and notice that the trainers seated to the side remain straight faced and unmoved.

'Maybe they've heard it before,' says Robert with an equally straight face.

(More laughter and applause for the person that just shared)

'But what if it's not someone's fault? I still think Richard isn't to blame for having his car stolen,' says Fran.

Fran is a large girl, around thirty years old. She has dark hair that is short but curls around her face. Earlier, she had given a brilliant description of being in her box. She doesn't look anything like her voice sounded.

'People are always going round looking for something or someone to blame,' says Robert. 'It's easy to feel that you don't have to take responsibility when you can find something or someone to blame. The toast is burnt, blame the toaster. Little Johnny bumps into the chair, blame the chair. There is no blame when you take responsibility and

109

when you take responsibility your lives start to work. The fact of the matter is that Richard chooses to own a car. He knows there are risks attached to car ownership. One of which is the possibility that someone might steal it. He knows that cars get stolen when they are left unattended but he chooses to leave his car to go shopping with his fiancée. He has to take responsibility for his decisions, his actions.'

(Applause for Fran)

'I had my briefcase stolen when I was in London last year. It was snatched from me. I didn't know it was going to happen. A can't see how I can take responsibility for that,' says James.

'Do briefcases never get stolen in London then?' Robert asks him.

(Laughter)

'Of course but how would I know that it would happen to me?'

'You don't know that someone is going to steal *your* briefcase on any particular day. But if you take responsibility for being in the world you must be aware of the fact that you have chosen to go, with a briefcase, to London, a place where briefcases get stolen.'

'I had to go to London to deliver some important papers.'

'You chose to go to London without a bodyguard, without armed support.'

(Laughter)

'You could have sent the documents by secure courier. There were plenty of choices but you made your choice and now you won't take responsibility for it. However, when you start to take responsibility you become aware of the nature of choice. Your decisions become those of a considered, more powerful person. Your choices are sharper and the outcome is always more satisfactory. As a consequence of taking responsibility you take more care of your briefcase and funnily enough, you are less likely to have it stolen. Thank you James.'

James sits. He has an expression on his face like his mental cogs are whirring round.

(Applause for James)

'But if his case is stolen, *why* should he take responsibility for it?' asks Pat. 'I'm still not getting it.'

'The Zen Buddhists tell a story,' says Robert. 'One night a monk is sitting in the temple cleaning the golden gong that stands just inside the entrance. He sees a man approaching carrying a large club. He continues cleaning. The man steps inside the temple and demands money. The monk tells him that there is no money in the temple. The man looks down at the gong and says he will take that instead. The monk tells him that he'll be finished cleaning it in a minute then he can have it. After a minute or so the monk hands the gong to the man who runs off.

In the morning there is uproar in the village. Many people are complaining that their houses were robbed by a man with a club.

"Was the temple robbed?" they ask the Monk.

The monk says, "No."

"Where is the temple's golden gong," they ask.

The monk says that he gave it to a man the evening before.

"He said he wanted money but we didn't have any so I gave him the gong," he tells them.'

Robert pauses for a few seconds.

'You see. Not only do you have to take responsibility for choosing to place yourself in position where your goods might be stolen but you also have the choice as to whether you experience them as being stolen.'

'OK. I'm getting it now,' says Pat.

(Applause)

111

'What about fate? What if our acts are preordained?'

It is Simon. He is still wearing the jacket with the elbow patches.

'By whom?' asks Robert.

'Well God. What if God has determined our paths.'

'God? What's *she* got to do with it?' asks Robert.

(Some laughter)

'I believe that God exists and that it is possible he has mapped out our fates for us?'

'Look Simon,' Robert says. 'I doubt very much if you know anything about her. I bet you wouldn't recognise her if she came up and blew in your ear.'

(Some laughter).

'I have had an experience of God.'

'Describe your experience.'

'Once, whilst in prayer, I experienced God as an omnipotent and all-knowing being. Surely it is possible that he has preordained everything that we do.'

'Oh great!' exclaims Robert. 'Now we've got someone blaming God. Well done Simon. Simon has an experience of something he thinks might be God, he adds a belief to that experience and hey presto! It's God's fault.'

'I'm not blaming God.'

'You are Arsehole. By saying that God has pre-ordained everything, you are saying that you have no choice, that something else has chosen everything for you and that means that it can never be your fault. You can say that it is fate, so it is not my fault, it is God's will.'

'I'm not blaming God.'

Simon's face has reddened, his voice is raised.

'Yes, and that wall over there is yellow not blue.'

Robert points to one of the blue walls.

'Well I have my faith,' says Simon.

'You are creating your experience of faith. You create your experience of God.'

Robert looks over the entire group of trainees.

'You can all go on blaming who you like but it won't work. Now that you have been introduced to *responsibility* you'll find that it will become harder and harder to blame everyone and everything for what you create.'

(Applause for Simon)

'This morning I went to the station and the train was cancelled. We had to go to the next station by bus and get the train from there. The journey took longer and I might have been late but it wouldn't have been my fault,' says Rachel.

Rachel is dark and small and pretty. She is dressed in black trousers and a black polo neck jumper.

'You weren't late though,' says Robert.

'I was lucky.'

'If you had been late it would have been your responsibility. You know there is a possibility that the train can be delayed. It would have meant that you hadn't left enough time to cover the eventualities of the journey.'

Rachel sits.

(Applause)

'What if someone has chucked a nail onto the road and I get a puncture on the way in and I'm late. Is that my fault?' asks Matt.

'Yes because you know there is a possibility of getting a puncture and you should have left enough time to cover the eventuality. It depends on your intent. If you intend to be somewhere on time then you

113

will be there on time.'

'But we can't take into consideration every possible eventuality can we.'

'Let me put this to you. If I said to you that I will give you a million pounds and all you have to do to receive it is be at my house on Tuesday morning at nine o'clock. There's one proviso though. If you're late by even one second, you will not get the million pounds. Would you be on time?'

'I'd be there Monday night camping out to make sure I was on time,' says Matt through a laugh.

(Laughter)

'Of course you would,' says Robert. 'You would make sure to take responsibility for any eventualities by arriving early. It's easy when there is a big pay off like a million quid. But if it's just being on time for work or for a date or for the seminar; well it's not a million is it. You don't see it as being as important so you choose not to apply as much intent to arriving early. Your choice, your responsibility. You see, you choose the level of intent that you apply to your acts. If you do something then you intended to do it. If you don't do something you didn't intend to do it. It's integrity. If you say you're going to do something, do it. If you say you're going to turn up at nine, turn up at nine.'

(Applause for Matt)

'Life *is* black and white. If you do something, then you intended to do it. If you don't do something, then you didn't intend to do it. When you take responsibility you are aware of the level of intent that you are applying to your actions.'

Robert stands in the aisle between the two rows of seats.

'And while we're on the subject of integrity. Who here has broken an agreement?'

114

Robert waits.

'Come on. If you've chucked your enlightenment notebook and pencil away we're not really going to charge you.'

(Laughter)

'I had a splitting headache when I got home last night and I took an aspirin,' says Amanda.

(Applause)

'When I got home my girlfriend had a bottle of wine open. She was waiting up for me. I had a glass,' says Ray.

(Applause)

'See,' says Robert. 'It is all about integrity. Why keep an agreement if you don't consider it important. It's only an aspirin, only a glass of wine. If you took responsibility for being on the seminar and committed yourself to finishing it and getting something from it then the agreements you made would look more important to you.'

'I forgot my notebook,' says Celia. 'Well, I chucked it away maliciously actually.'

Celia is smiling.

(Laughter and applause)

'If you were committed to completing the seminar and took responsibility for choosing to be here then you would take responsibility and not break your agreements. It's like when people don't complete what they start. They leave things half finished, give up on a project or put off finishing something. You can invent for yourself a million excuses why you don't have to complete something when you are not taking responsibility.'

'Yes but there's a difference between Celia's enlightenment notebook and James' case,' says Sam.

'There is no difference,' Robert interrupts. 'The enlightenment

115

notebooks don't *really* have magic powers you know.'

Robert's tone of voice is one like you might use if talking to a child.

(Laughter)

'We said that to make an illustration regarding taking responsibility and not leaving stuff lying around.'

'No,' says Sam. 'The difference is that Celia was told not to lose the notebook or leave it behind. James wasn't forewarned.'

'But when you take responsibility you consider your options and use all of the information available. That is how you expect the unexpected. You then make your choice and having made that choice you take responsibility for the outcome.'

Robert is standing looking relaxed.

'And as I said. It is likely that James' case would not have been stolen.'

(Applause for Sam)

'I get it,' says James.

When I look over at James I see that he still has his hand in the air and has a huge grin on his face.

(Applause for James)

The sharing goes backwards and forwards. Points are raised and discussed, some of the trainees, like James, *get* what Robert is saying regarding responsibility, others have yet to catch on. Some don't agree with the proposition at all.

'I can't accept that I have to take responsibility for everything that happens to me,' says Jaclyn. 'You can't expect people to take responsibility, for example, if they are the victim of circumstance.'

116

'A victim of circumstance?' Robert asks.

'Yes. Take my sister for example. She is abused by her husband. How can that be her fault? Why should she take responsibility for that?'

'Is the abuse physical or mental or both?' asks Robert.

'Mostly physical.'

'She should take responsibility and leave.'

'Why should she leave? She is the victim in this. Besides there's the children.'

'If your sister took responsibility for her life she wouldn't be a victim. She could ask, or tell, her husband to go. If he refuses she should go and take the children with her. If she chooses to stay then she knows her husband may be violent and abusive. It is her choice to stay and be abused. People choose to be a victim.'

'She hasn't got anywhere to go.'

'She could stay with you.'

'We don't have the room.'

'Of course you do. You just don't want to compromise. It wouldn't be for long. If her house burnt down you'd put her up, wouldn't you.'

'Of course.'

'But you don't think your sister getting knocked about is a serious as having her house burnt down?'

'It isn't about me. It's about my sister and her husband.'

'It is about you. If you took responsibility you would offer to let her stay at your place until she is sorted out. Alternatively you could support her and help her find somewhere else. There are other options, other choices. When you take responsibility, your actions become stronger and more decisive. You are no longer a victim. The fact remains that your sister's husband is a violent moron but you both have to take

117

responsibility for that. Your sister, because she should be more careful about her choice of husbands, and you, because you choose to care.'

'I still don't think it is our fault,' says Jaclyn.

'It is not about blame. If you assume responsibility for being in the world then you must take responsibility for your own choices. That includes the experience you get around a given circumstance.'

Robert is standing close to where Jaclyn is standing.

'What do you get around your sister's situation?'

'I feel sad for her and angry about him.'

'In this case, your experience around your sisters' circumstance is grief and anger. You are creating those emotions. Your beliefs around your sister, the nature of domestic violence, the raising of children and so on and so forth give rise to your choice of emotion, of experience. Other people with different beliefs will likely get a different experience. It is your creation and as such, your responsibility.'

'OK,' Jaclyn says.

From her voice, I note that her intonation is tinged with a tone of reluctant acceptance.

(Applause for Jaclyn)

Robert walks back onto the low stage and stands next to the lectern.

'I am going to add another two levels of base experiences to our chart.'

Robert flicks the page back on the chart to where he had written

Apathy

Grief

Fear

Anger

Pride

118

Joy

He writes, next to the word Joy, / Satisfaction and then, underneath, Responsibility. So it now reads:

Apathy

Grief

Fear

Anger

Pride

Joy / Satisfaction

Responsibility

'I'm going to leave those two hanging there for a while. They will come up shortly but for the meantime just give a bit of consideration to what they might be.'

Robert steps back down off of the stage.

'I mentioned *commitment* earlier. I want to talk a little about what is it and how do we create it.'

Hands go up but Robert waives them away.

'I'm going to tell you what it is then you can share whatever it is you want to share,' he says.

He walks along in front of the first row of chairs. He is holding a piece of paper in his hand. He looks down at it and reads.

'The dictionary definition of commitment is: an undertaking to which one is bound, a pledge, to incur a duty, an obligation. The meaning that I am concerned with is this last one.'

Robert holds up the piece of paper.

'An unflinching desire to reach or attain ones goal.'

He taps the paper with his finger.

'Give me some examples of commitment in this respect.'

'I'm committed to making some money,' says Matt. 'One of the

119

reasons I'm here is to get my life together, you know, financially. To get a job and get some money.'

(Applause)

'I want to be able to decide whether to leave my husband,' says Cally.

Cally is another person that I hadn't noticed before. She is small with curly blonde hair. She has an American or Canadian accent.

'I came over here from Canada to study and met my husband. We've been together for five years and married for two. He doesn't want to work, he has become a slob. I don't know whether to try and help him buck his ideas up or just leave him.'

Cally makes a sort of take off – flying gesture with her hand as she says, 'leave him'.

'Are you committed to finding an answer to your dilemma?' asks Robert.

'I guess I am,' she says.

(Applause)

'I'm committed to finishing this seminar even though I am tired and my bum is sore,' says Marjory.

(Laughter)

'That's exactly it,' says Robert.

He points to Marjory.

'Marjory is creating commitment by including all of the things that she is experiencing as part of the process of attaining her goal. You create commitment by including all of the obstacles that arise as proof that you are proceeding towards your goal. The obstacle of Marjory's sore behind wouldn't arise unless she was still in the room doing the seminar. It is validation that she is preceding towards her goal. Yes Joe.'

'So you're saying that when I'm at work and I get an unfair

120

bollocking from my boss that it is proof that I'm proceeding towards my goal.'

'It depends,' says Robert. 'What is your goal?'

'To get my boss's job because I know I can do it better than him. If I can't get on in the company then I'll leave.'

'Then, if you have a commitment towards getting your boss's job, it *is* proof. If you weren't working with your boss you wouldn't be getting involved with a confrontation with him. You must also include your cop out statement of, "if I can't get what I want I'll quit," as an obstacle that proves you are proceeding towards your goal.'

Everyone laughs when Robert does a perfect impersonation of Joe saying, 'If I can't get what I want I'll quit'.

'You create those shitty sentiments as part of your racket and they will inevitably surface as you proceed towards your goal.'

(Applause)

'You create commitment by recognising and including these obstacles as proof that you are proceeding towards your goal,' Robert reiterates.

'I'm committed to finding a new path in my life but I have to look after my kids. How do I include that as an obstacle?'

'We're back to responsibility,' says Robert. 'You don't have to look after your kids. You choose to. You don't have to do anything. If you are committed to finding a new life you will need to include the obstacle of you not taking responsibility for your decisions as proof that you are proceeding towards your goal.'

Robert, once again, walks between the two blocks of chairs.

'*Responsibility* is an insidious thing,' he says.

He has returned to the stage and is standing in front of the lectern.

121

'Once you have been introduced to it your bodies realize the truth of it. You will never be able to return to your ways of not taking responsibility for your decisions, for not taking responsibility for being in the world. It will nag at you. You will know deep down that there can be no getting away from it. Oh you'll try and wriggle out of it, many of you will try heroically to resist it but it will do you no good. You are fucked!'

(Laughter)

'Nothing you can do about it however hard you try.'

With this Robert calls a break for forty five minutes. We all go through our break routines. It is three thirty in the afternoon. I go to the cafe around the corner with Marjory and Brian to get a snack. It has been a long session but strangely, a much easier one to get through. When I mention this, Marjory says that she thought it was particularly tough and challenging. Brian says that he had trouble staying awake. This seems odd to me because they both appeared to be quite lively during the last session.

We are back in the room. We have, as usual, been relieved of our coats, bags and watches and been handed our name tags. The trainers have resumed their positions and maintain their previous stoic demeanours. I notice that the lectern and flip chart have been moved to the left side of the stage.

We are all seated. Kim enters. She walks to the front and stands on the edge of the stage. She is dressed, as before, in a smart business suit with a crisp white blouse underneath. She stands as if she is waiting for something.

After a few seconds the door opens and one of the trainees

hurries in and takes a seat. It is Ray. He raises his hand, stands and says sorry for being late. Kim beckons him to the front and Ray takes a seat. His ruddy face is a shade redder.

'So fuck all of us then,' says Kim. 'You couldn't be bothered to be on time. We can all wait for you because you're so important and we can all fuck off.'

The room is very quiet. Kim looks livid. I can't tell if it an act or not.

Ray puts his hand up.

'I'm sorry,' he says again. 'I misread my watch. Entirely my fault, sorry.'

'Nobody does anything that they don't want to do Ray,' says Kim. 'When you choose not be on time you are saying, "fuck you," to all of us. Normally you wouldn't have been allowed back in but this time I'm going to let you stay in the room.'

Ray nods his head contritely. Kim signals him to sit.

(Applause)

I am not sure if the applause is acknowledgement for Ray or relief that he wasn't thrown out. It is probably a bit of both.

'For me, not being on time is one of the worst rackets. Along with losing stuff. You don't have to be late all the time. You don't have to lose stuff either. It's a fucking racket. It's part of a controlling racket. I'm late. You can all wait for me.'

Kim is prowling up and down in front of the stage.

'And losing things. Oh! I've lost my bag. All my stuff is in there. Focus on me. Well fucking great. Lose your bag, create a drama.'

Kim shakes her head.

'No,' she says. 'Not with me.'

Everyone is quiet. I sense that most of the trainees are feeling

123

uncomfortable. It is like being back at school and the whole classroom is in trouble.

'There are a few people in here who need to get off their rackets, take responsibility and show some integrity.'

Kim walks down the aisle between the two rows of chairs.

'I want us to discuss what giving *one hundred percent* means,' she continues. 'Firstly, I want to make it clear that I hate the expression *one hundred and ten percent*. When someone says to me, "I'm going to give it one hundred and ten percent," I always think to myself, what the fuck does that mean? What is one hundred and ten percent? If you can give one hundred and ten percent why not one hundred and twenty percent or two hundred percent or a million percent. It's meaningless. It's meaningless because one hundred percent is the maximum. One hundred percent is an expression of the maximum amount. There can be no more. A glass can't be one hundred and ten percent full. If it is full it is one hundred percent full.'

Kim is walking up and down the aisle slowly. Everyone is concentrating and paying attention. I imagine that no one wants to get into a verbal exchange with Kim right now. Not after what Ray received.

'Who can give me an example of a time when they thought they gave one hundred percent. Yes Cally.'

'When I was younger I was really into athletics. It was difficult for me because I'm not that tall but I remember once, in a race with some much bigger girls I beat them. I believe I gave one hundred percent at that time.'

'What was your experience afterwards? What did you *get*?' asks Kim.

'Oh, satisfaction,' says Cally.

Cally makes her mouth into an upside down smile and nods her

124

head.

'Yes sir. I felt great.'

(Applause)

'I always try and give one hundred percent. At work, for example, I am totally focused on what I'm doing,' says Peter.

Peter is the tinnitus sufferer who had been in the navy.

'Sometimes though, you get worn down. Through people not noticing how much you're putting in or not working as hard.'

'Give me a specific incidence,' says Kim.

'Last week, for instance, I stayed late. I wanted to finish up a report. I worked really hard. But when I handed it in I hardly got any thanks. It was de-motivating.'

'What did you *get*?' asks Kim.

'Grief, I suppose and anger.'

(Applause)

'Sometimes when I'm acting and everyone is giving their best, everything falls into place. It is intensely satisfying,' says Kate.

(Applause)

People stand up and share. Some share about giving one hundred percent, others comment on what someone has shared. A few of the anecdotes are to do with people's work some are sports related, one or two people tell of undertaking simple tasks but doing them really well.

'You have been sharing about times when you thought you were giving one hundred percent,' says Kim. 'Let us try and understand what the components of giving one hundred percent are. Has anyone heard the expression *he or she was playing out of his mind*?' asks Kim.

A few hands go up and people acknowledge that they had heard the expression.

'What is the experience when that happens? Can anyone tell me of an experience they've had like that.'

'Sometimes when I'm playing the piano I am only aware of what I'm doing. I'm really in the groove, in the zone,' says Ray.

'I was somehow expecting a greater amount of sharing from you Ray,' says Kim. 'I was waiting for you to start to seek approval. To try and get back in my good books.'

(Nervous laughter)

'He's right though,' she continues. 'In the zone, in the groove, out of your mind. It means you have *nothing going on*, no rackets, no beliefs. You are just doing. It is then that you are giving one hundred percent.'

Kim has stopped pacing. She is standing in front of the stage again.

'When you assume responsibility for your decisions it is easier to give one hundred percent. To give everything to whatever task you choose to undertake.'

'When you take responsibility and you drop your beliefs and concentrate on what is real, namely, your experience, you will find yourselves proceeding with *nothing going on*. No beliefs, no rackets just what *is*. If you have given one hundred percent then you may be lucky and experience *satisfaction*.'

Kim walks to halfway down the aisle between the two blocks of chairs.

'So,' she says. 'We are going to do a little process that will enable you all to give one hundred percent. To have *nothing going on*. The process involves a little performance. Everyone will take part. There are two routines that we want you to perform. We are going to split you

126

into females and males. The first routine is the song: *How much is that doggy in the window*. This will be performed as if you were a sugar sweet little girl in a frilly dress. Like Shirley Temple, with all the coquettish, little girl expressions and movements. The second is called, *Fee fi fo fum*. This will be performed as if you are a big, evil smelling, hairy, ogre. Once again, with all of the pertinent movements and expressions.'

There is some nervous laughter along with a rising sense of anticipation. Many of the trainees fidget on their seats and sit up straight.

'One of the trainers will give you a demonstration. First, *How much is that doggy in the window*. Oh, I forgot to mention,' Kim continues, 'the boys will be doing *How much is that doggy* and the girls will be doing *Fee fi fo fum*.'

(Groans and more nervous laughter)

'Nick will give a demonstration for the boys. When he has finished you must acknowledge him.'

Nick strides purposefully from the back of the room and up on to the stage. He has the same expressionless demeanour as he turns to face us, his audience. He then proceeds to give the most fantastic energised performance of *How much is that doggy in the window* as if he was a young flirtatious and coquettish ten year old girl in a frilly dress.

'How much is that doggy in the window, the one with the waggerly tail. How much is that doggy in the window, I do hope that doggy's for sale.'

He sings the verses through twice, in a high giggly voice. He puts his hands together at the side of his face and purses his lips and widens his eyes as he sings. Best of all though, when he sings *the one with the waggerly tail*, he turns around and wiggles his bottom from side to side. There is much laughter during the performance, mostly from the girls. The performance is acknowledged with loud applause. Nick's face

127

returns to one devoid of expression. He stands for a moment, receives the applause and leaves.

'Elizabeth will now give a demonstration for the girls,' says Kim.

Elizabeth, another of the trainers, strides to the stage in the same way as Nick. She stands for a moment and then crouches with her arms curved and her hands formed into fists. As she recites the lines she stamps her feet from side to side and makes fearsome facial grimaces.

'Fe fi fo fum I smell the blood of an Englishman. Be he alive or be he dead, I'll grind his bones to make my bread.'

At the end, after she has said, 'make my bread,' she lets out a deep fearsome roar. 'Arrghh!'

Once again, there is loud applause and much laughter, this time, mostly from the boys. In the same way as Nick, Elizabeth's expressionless demeanour returns. She stands until the applause has finished and then departs.

'I want you to come up in groups of five. I want five males up first and I want five females waiting to come up. As soon as the females go up I want another group of five males to wait at the side. We need to get a production line going or we could be here all night.'

Kim is organising the logistics of getting more than one hundred and thirty people to perform.

'I want you to perform individually within your group. If you do not give one hundred percent in your performance you will have to repeat it on your own until you do.'

Kim takes up a position in the aisle between the two banks of chairs. She nods to the trainers who start to direct the groups of trainees onto the low stage. The first group performs a rather limp rendition.

'That was pathetic,' remarks Kim. 'Do it again. All of you and this time I want to see your inner little girls shine out. I want to see those little coquettish hand movements and most of all, I want to see you wiggle your tush. When you have finished I want you to stand and receive the acknowledgement. Remember, *nothing going on.*'

She turns to those of us seated.

'And I want more support from you. When they come to the line, *the one with the waggerly tail*, and they turn and wiggle their bottoms, I want you all to shout *Woof Woof*! Got it?'

(Laughter)

The first five lambs to the slaughter start again. They sing and act like little girls and duly waggle their tails to shouts of 'Woof Woof!' When they finish there is loud applause.

'OK! Better. You can step down,' says Kim. 'NEXT,' she says loudly.

The five waiting females go up to be replaced at the side by another set of five nervous looking males.

'Fe fi fo fum, I smell the blood of an Englishman.'

The five females give an excellent rendition of the rhyme. They really look like ogres and finish with a loud 'Arrghh!'

As we acknowledge them, they all stand and receive our applause. All except Amanda who turns and grins at the others in a congratulatory manner.

'Very good,' says Kim, 'except for Amanda who was still on her racket. You can all step down. Amanda, you can do it again.'

Amanda does it again but doesn't impress Kim. She tries again and again. After the fourth or fifth time we are all willing her to give a *one hundred percent* performance. Eventually she does. There is loud applause.

'Next,' says Kim.

The next five go up onto the stage, once again to be replaced at the side by another five waiting. The production line is in full motion.

I work out that the average performance, including people having to do it again, must take around four to five minutes except, that is, when there are bouts of sharing. These are mostly directed by Kim. She may, for example, ask someone what they thought of a particular performance. These interludes, I estimate, take the average up to seven or eight minutes. I think to myself that this is going to take at least three hours.

'Matt. Did you think Frank gave one hundred percent?'

'Err! Yes. I thought he did OK.'

'BULLSHIT,' Kim shouts. 'DID YOU GET THAT HE WAS GIVING ONE HUNDRED PERCENT?'

'Well! No,' says Matt. 'Sorry Frank,' he adds.

'Don't say sorry to him, he should apologise to you. He's the one not giving. He's the one delaying your dinner.'

Kim turns to Frank.

'Do it again Frank.'

Frank repeats the performance.

'Yes,' says Marjory enthusiastically when asked if Frank managed it this time.

'I thought so too,' says Kim. 'Next.'

(Applause for Frank)

Up on to the low stage we go to perform and in some cases perform twice or more, until Kim is satisfied that we have given one hundred percent.

'Fe fi fo fum...Arrghh!'

'How much is that doggie in the window, the one with the waggerly tail.'

'Woof Woof.'

When everyone has performed Kim walks up onto the stage. The trainers return to their positions. Kim has a wry smile.

'I've seen better,' she says. 'My favourite was Brian. You may have a future as a squeaky little girl after all.'

(Laughter)

'And Cally. No wonder her husband doesn't want to do anything. What an ogre.'

(More laughter)

Kim spends a little more time poking fun. I speculate that she is waiting for us to calm down.

'On the whole most of you gave one hundred percent. All done without procrastination as well. You know what I mean about procrastination?'

Kim waits a few moments.

'Putting things off,' offers Sally.

(Applause)

'Putting things off,' Kim repeats. 'You know, when you need to do something and you say to yourself, I'll just have a cigarette before I do that, or a cup of tea or something to eat. Rather than getting straight on with the thing you need to do.'

(Some laughter)

'I know exactly what you mean. I often do it before I have to make a phone call,' says James. 'I don't know why I do it but nine times out of ten I make up an excuse to delay the call. It's probably because I

131

don't like talking business over the phone.'

'It's because you are frightened,' says Kim. 'You are experiencing fear. It could be fear of communicating, fear of rejection, any number of things. Once again, what you need to do is acknowledge your experience and don't try to avoid it with that cigarette or that biscuit. Go with the experience without trying to change it.'

(Applause for James)

Kim steps over to the lectern and starts to organise the papers that she has there.

'We're going to take a break now,' she says. 'One hour and thirty minutes.'

There is a collective enthusiasm for Kim's announcement. We hand in our badges, pick up our stuff and leave the room. Outside, it is seven forty five in the evening.

I go to have something to eat with Jed, Marjory, Celia and Greg. We are in high spirits after the performance. Marjory makes a comment about how the energy levels went up during the performance and how the group of trainees had 'come together'.

'It seems as if we are all supporting one and other,' says Celia. 'Like we want to help each other come through this.'

I too have noticed a willingness by the trainees to support someone who struggles but acts honestly with nothing going on.

'It feels like we are all fuh family,' says Greg.

I am not alone in noticing that Greg's stutter is much less pronounced. As he speaks the others smile at him, almost like proud parents. He is aware of it too.

We return at ten past nine. As we enter the room it is clear that the trainers' demeanour is sterner than we have seen before. This time, they not only relieve us of our watches, bags and coats but other items. They empty our pockets and take our wallets, purses and money along with all items of jewellery like rings, earrings, chains and bangles. These are put into envelopes and placed at the back of the room with our extraneous articles of clothing, that have also been removed, like belts, neck scarves, jackets, cardigans and pullovers. There is the occasional objection which is waived aside. It feels like we have been caught off guard after returning from our dinner break with full stomachs, empty bladders and nicotine cravings satisfied. In addition, the room has changed. The chairs have been stacked at the side and there are a couple of long bench like tables that have been placed in line together. They stand at the side of the room and at right angles to the stage. They are perhaps fifteen or sixteen feet long by four feet wide and three feet tall. There is a chair at each end of the table benches. We are told to stand in rows at the side, in front of the stacked chairs, and wait in silence. Needless to say, these proceedings generate an air of apprehension amongst the trainees.

'We are going to do a process to see how you get on without your props.'

Kim is standing in front of the two table benches.

'We have removed all of those little things that keep you comfortable and we are going to get you to just be with some other people, like I said, without your props.'

Eight of the trainers walk to the benches and, using the chair at the end, climb up. They stand in a line, their backs facing the room. The remainder of the trainers take positions below, at either side of the benches, in front and behind, as if they were there to catch anyone that

133

fell.

'You will come up onto the tables, eight at a time, and stand facing a trainer. You will keep your hands to your side. Let them hang loosely as the trainers' hands are now. You will then connect with the trainer in front of you. That is, you will look into their eyes and they will look into yours. There will be nowhere to hide and none of your usual props and no chance for you to use your usual rackets.'

There are a couple of objections.

'I'm not confident about standing on that table,' says Miranda.

'Don't worry. Someone will be there to stop you falling.'

It is hardly a re-assurance but bravely Miranda climbs up with seven others.

As the trainees stand Kim speaks.

'Stand still and don't fidget. Look them in the eyes, connect. Let your hands hang loosely at your sides.'

As she speaks a couple of the trainers, who are stationed below, adjust peoples' hands ensuring that they are positioned at their sides.

'You will stay connected with the person opposite you until I say to finish,' says Kim.

From down below, the *connection* lasts for a few minutes. It seems much longer when you are up there though. As the trainees stand it is evident that some find it extremely uncomfortable, to the extent that their legs are shaking. One of the trainees, Ray, tries to rub his hands together but is prevented from doing so by the trainer below who re-adjusts his hands to the side. I notice one or two trainees have tears on their faces as they climb down.

'Don't smile,' Kim orders Tania. 'Get rid of that stupid grin and drop your fucking racket. Just be up there. No hiding behind your cutesy, aren't I lovely, smile.'

134

Tania stops smiling, her legs start to shake a little and her lip begins to wobble. She too, is crying when she steps down.

I notice, when it is my turn, that I have a compulsion to rub the back of my head. I remember that I do this often when I am in an uncomfortable situation. I had noticed others doing similar things such as Tania's smile and Ray trying to rub his hands together. It occurs to me that there is probably an element of compulsion involved in their actions as well. In fact it becomes clear that most of us feel the need to do something with our hands. This process must be designed to stimulate these automatic responses and then deny us their comfort.

'Take your hand out of your pocket. Didn't you listen? Can't you follow the instructions? Stand still. Look! Engage with your partner. I want you to just *be* up there.'

Some of the trainees appear to handle the process better than others. A number of the trainees' legs shake, there are a few wobbly lips and some tears. I notice that those who are standing, waiting to take their turn, look increasingly anxious and those who have completed the process and stand waiting for the others to finish have retained a similar serious and concerned expression.

When everyone has taken their turn we are directed to find a space on the floor and sit down. In all, the process has taken perhaps one and a half hours.

We are seated on the floor. The door at the rear opens, and to my slight surprise Robert enters the room. He too carries an expression that is sterner than usual. He walks to the side of the room and looks down at us

135

on the floor. He is immaculately dressed and looks completely fresh, as usual. We, on the other hand, look on the point of exhaustion, which is not surprising given the long morning session, the afternoon of the one hundred percent performances and the last process.

'By now I hope that you are able to identify your experience,' he says. 'What was your overriding experience during that process?'

Robert is standing in front of us. We are still seated on the floor.

'There is no need to stand when you share,' he adds.

'Fear,' says Marjory. 'When I was made to stand up there I felt very uncomfortable and I realised that I was experiencing fear. I didn't know why I should be afraid just because I was in an uncomfortable situation.'

(Applause)

'Yes, fear for me as well,' says a male voice.

(Applause)

I am unable to see who it was from my position. Also, oddly, I find it difficult to applaud whilst seated on the floor.

'Fear is one of the base emotions,' says Robert. 'It is one that you experience a great deal of the time but up to now you haven't recognised it or haven't been aware it is fear that you are experiencing. When you do become aware of your experience of fear you try to avoid it.'

Robert walks between us. We remain seated on the floor.

'I want you to get in touch with the thing that you are most afraid of and share it. Come on. Who's first?'

'Spiders,' says Mani.

Her name badge spells Mani but her name is pronounced Marnie. She is a slightly built girl with a long face and dishwater blonde hair.

136

'I hate spiders.'

'What do you hate about them,' asks Robert.

'I don't know. I just hate them.'

'Is it the way they move or the way they look?'

'Both. I hate everything about them. Even thinking about them or talking about them gives me the creeps.'

'Identify one specific incidence where you encountered them.'

Mani hesitates for a moment.

'I remember we had an old garage at the end of our garden. I went in there, out of curiosity I think, and I walked straight through a web. It was awful. It was all over me. There were spiders. They were in the web and then I saw that some were on my arm and then I felt them on my face and my neck.'

Mani tucks her chin into her chest, raises her shoulders up and shakes her head.

'Erghh!' she exclaims. 'It was horrible. I ran out trying to brush them off and I accidently squashed one on my arm. I hate to even think about it.'

'And can you recall what you experienced?'

'I found them....'

Mani hesitates for a moment, trying to find the word.

'Repulsive,' she continues. 'It was fear but also a sort of disgust.'

'Who else?'

(Applause for Mani)

'Velvet. I hate the feeling of it on my skin,' says Ray. 'From my earliest memory I have disliked it.'

'Can you recall an incident with velvet,' asks Robert.

'My two brothers threw a velvet curtain over me when I was five

137

or six years old. They knew I didn't like the stuff. It was well cruel.'

Ray gives a short chuckle that comes out like a snort.

'They were older than me but I caught them and hit them when I got free.'

'What was your experience when you were under the velvet?'

'I was terrified while I was under there but when I got free I was angry.'

(Applause)

'Death,' says James. 'I am afraid of dying.'

'Specifically James. What is it around death that you are frightened of?'

'There being nothing there I suppose. It being the end. No more consciousness. No more me.'

(Applause)

'I am afraid of dying alone,' says Marjory. 'Not death itself but having a slow lingering death and there being no one to help or be with me.'

(Applause)

'Yes, Ian,' says Robert.

Ian is well over six feet tall with short blonde hair. He has not shared much throughout the previous days. He is quiet but easily noticeable due to his height and muscular frame. He doesn't look like he'd be afraid of anything.

'I have a fear of being incapacitated. Going blind or not being able to walk,' says Ian. 'When I was in the army I saw a couple of the lads after they were injured. I don't know what I would do. I suppose I am afraid that my life would be over.'

(Applause)

There follows sharing about things, items or circumstances where the trainees have experienced fear. With some Robert gets them to identify a specific incidence when they experienced their fear.

'I want each of you to visualize a situation where you are experiencing fear,' Robert is saying. 'I want you to revisit your worst fear. I want you to experience it again. You are going to undergo a cathartic experience by imagining yourself in that situation again. For example, you Marjory must imagine yourself dying alone. Put yourself in that situation. Are you on your bed or on the floor? Are you inside a room or outside? Get in touch with what you are experiencing. What are your bodily sensations?'

Robert is walking amongst us as he speaks.

'If anybody feels like they need to vomit during this process put your hand up and one of the trainers will supply you with a bag.'

He directs us to lie on the floor with our eyes closed.

'Mani, you are back in the shed. You have run in to the web, the spider's nest. You come outside you are covered in spiders. Ian, you are incapacitated. Place yourself in that situation. Where are you? Imagine the scene. Get in touch with what you are experiencing.'

I have my eyes closed. I can hear a few sobs and groans along with the odd exclamation like 'Urghh!' or 'Aghh!' I can hear people moving amongst us. Robert reminds us of the fear that we have shared and encourages us to get in touch with our experience of that fear. We have spent perhaps ten or fifteen minutes getting in touch with our individual fears. We are lying in the same way, still with our eyes closed.

'Next,' says Robert. 'I want you to pretend to be terrified of the person lying next to you.'

'Imagine them to be associated with the fear that you have just experienced. You are so terrified of the person next to you that you want to scream,' he says. 'Scream.'

There is some screaming.

'Louder,' says Robert. 'SCREAM,' he shouts.

(Loud screams)

'Now, you are terrified of everyone in the room. You are in danger. SCREAM!' he shouts.

(More loud screaming)

'They're coming to get you. The whole room is about to jump on you. SCREAM!' shouts Robert again.

There is a barrage of loud screaming that increases to a crescendo. It seems to go on for three or four minutes. My throat is sore. It feels like I have swallowed a sheet of oven hot sandpaper.

Finally, Robert calms everyone down.

'OK, open your eyes and sit up,' he says.

Robert is standing at the front.

'Yep!' he says. 'You are all scared shitless of everyone. You're scared of the person next to you. You're scared of the people at the party. You're scared of the people on the bus. You're scared of your boss, you're scared of the person behind the counter in the shop. You are scared shitless.'

Robert walks up and down, between the trainees who are dotted about on the floor of the room.

'Everywhere you go, everyone you meet. You are scared of them. In your lives, your predominant experience is fear. Fear of failure, fear of dying, fear of spiders. And, most noticeably, you are afraid of everyone around you.'

Robert has a glimmer of a smile appearing on his face.

'And you know the funny thing?' he says.

He pauses for a second.

'They are all scared of you. They are so scared they could crap their pants at any minute.'

(Laughter)

'The policeman that you are afraid of - he's scared of you. The man with the shaved head with *Fuck off* tattooed on his forehead – the most terrified of all – about to cack himself at any moment.'

(Laughter)

'Those people at the party, the ones that you are so scared of you have to grab a drink and knock it back or light up a cigarette - they are terrified of you. The waiter that you're so frightened of when you order your food - pissing himself with fear.'

(More laughter)

'The people you pass on the street that you daren't make eye contact with because you're so frightened of them – shitting themselves with fear – of you. Everyone is walking around absolutely terrified of everyone else.'

(Laughter)

'Everyone out there is frightened of everyone else. If there is a God he's got a mean sense of humour. Creating beings that are frightened of each other and then letting them loose so they can go round shitting themselves all of their lives.'

(Laughter)

'So, we are all frightened of each other and just to demonstrate it I want you to complete a process. When you leave here tonight, between now and Wednesday. I want you to walk up to a stranger and say, "Boo!" Just like that.'

141

(Laughter)

'You'll see how scared people are. Best not to pick on the bloke with *Fuck off* tattooed on his head though.'

(Laughter)

'He is shitting himself so much he's likely to get violent.'

As we laugh I notice that the trainers have relaxed their stern demeanours and are joining in with the laughter. Their whole mood has changed. It is as if they have taken off their severe masks and are now one of us.

'OK, you can go.'

Robert calls a close to the day. There is long, loud and enthusiastic applause as Robert leaves the room.

It takes quite a while for everyone to collect all of the items that were removed when we last entered the room. It is one thirty in the morning. I notice that many of the trainees look unsure as there are warm smiles and the odd word of approval from the trainers as we pick up our stuff. It is as if they expect them to revert to their stern demeanours at any moment.

I look around as we stream out. Everyone appears to be extremely energised. Most people are smiling. A few look completely shattered but still have wide bright eyes. People are holding their throats and laugh as they try to speak and nothing comes out. They nod and raise their hands to say goodbye. I too have almost completely lost my voice from the screaming.

The drive to drop off Jed then Marjory, Tania and Sarah is amusingly filled with our five barely audible, croaky voices.

I arrive home at three fifteen. I am unfazed at the prospect of getting up for work in four hours and not being able to speak.

Part 2

Self Improvement?
You Can't Polish a Turd

Middle Wednesday evening

We are seated in a different and smaller room this evening. There is no stage in this room. The seats are set out in one block this time. There are fewer trainers. They have retained their more pleasant and cheerful demeanours. They are still smartly dressed. We have not been relieved of our bags and watches. We have been handed our name tags. I imagine that they are a way of determining if everyone is present. The room is filled with an energised buzz. Everyone is on time, everyone has their enlightenment notebooks and pencils and no one is sitting next to anyone they know or have sat next to before.

The door opens and Kim enters. She walks to the front of the seats. There is long and sustained applause.

'Good evening.'

'Good evening,' we reply in unison.

The response is loud and enthusiastic, despite our still croaky voices.

'Did everyone enjoy their new found power over the last few days?' she asks.

(Laughter)

'It's good knowing everybody is scared of you isn't it. OK, let's have some sharing on what happened when you completed your *Boo* process.'

'I said it to a guy who was about my age as I was getting off the

Night Bus. He looked terrified. It was amazing,' says Matt.

There is loud, enthusiastic and energised applause to acknowledge the sharing.

'Ooh! You're all too good now,' jokes Kim.

(Laughter)

'Don't get too cocky. You haven't got it yet,' she says.

'I said it to a guy on the tube. He was so scared he got out and went into the carriage behind,' says Karen.

(Laughter)

Karen is the woman who looked like she was in her forties but was probably younger. This evening she did, in fact, look ten years younger than she had.

'I could see him looking at me through the partition door like I was a madwoman.'

(More laughter)

'I just want to add that I have had a fabulous three days since Sunday. I have had a spring in my step and I feel so much better about myself.'

(Applause)

'I said it to girl outside where I work,' says Celia. 'She was so scared that she went white. I felt so bad that I went to walk back to her and comfort her but she ran away.'

(Laughter and applause)

'I said it to a guy at the station,' Snick is standing. 'He just looked at me for a couple of seconds and then said, "Boo!" back to me. It really made me jump. He said to me, "I've done the seminar programme." He told me that the best is yet come.'

(Laughter and applause)

'He is right,' says Kim. 'Next weekend you will get it. Even those de-energised people who've been sleeping through the whole thing like Mark.'

Kim points to Mark who is sitting at the back with his eyes closed.

(Laughter)

Heads turn to look over at Mark. He opens his eyes. He is smiling. He stands.

'I've had such a busy few days. I haven't had much sleep,' he says.

'Did you say boo?' asks Kim.

'I was worried about saying it to be honest. Then I got in touch with my experience. I was frightened. I just went with it. I said it to someone who was coming out of a lift as I was getting in. I probably looked frightened when I said it to him which probably made it even scarier for him.'

(Laughter)

'He looked at me as if I was mad. I could tell that he was really scared though.'

(Applause)

We share our *Boo* stories. It is interesting that although many people acknowledge that they were frightened before saying it, they commented that knowing the other person was even more scared made the task easier. I imagine that courage is proceeding with a task even though you know you are frightened and carrying out that task without allowing your fear to impede your judgement or performance.

As well as their *Boo* experiences, a few trainees share that they have experienced heightened levels of energy since Sunday. It is something that I had noticed with myself. Kim tells us that what we

146

experience now is nothing to what they will get next weekend.

After the sharing Kim goes on to provide us with some details of what we can expect on the coming Saturday.

'We will be dealing with the real purpose of the seminar. Whatever your stated goals were, the purpose of the seminar boils down to one thing. Your stated goals are the drama. The reality is that you are going to transform your lives. Write this down in your notebooks. *The purpose of the seminar is to transform the barriers in my life to being one hundred percent satisfied by learning to experience my emotions accurately and clearly.*'

Everyone scribbles the words down.

'The world that you perceive is that which you choose to apprehend. You perceive the world through your senses.'

Kim writes this out on the white flip chart as she speaks.

'Your perception is filtered through your beliefs, which gives rise to your experience, your emotion. We have seen that if you suspend your beliefs and have nothing going on then you can fully experience your emotion. If you fully experience your emotion, without wanting to change it, the emotion can be transformed.'

Kim turns towards us.

'Got it?' she asks.

A hand goes up. It is Amanda.

'There's always one,' says Kim.

(Laughter)

Amanda is laughing too.

'I just wanted to ask if this is what getting it is.'

'No. But it is all leading up to it. You'll get the big tamale on Sunday,' says Kim.

147

I am oddly surprised to hear Kim using an American slang expression.

'I want to add that I feel so different to last week. I have started to take responsibility for being alive. It is amazing. That's why I asked about getting it. I can't believe I will feel better than I do,' says Amanda.

'Oh! Trust me,' says Kim. 'Next Sunday will blow your mind.'

(Applause for Amanda)

There is a noticeable change with Amanda. At first she looked frail and awkward. Now she appears to be full of confidence and energy.

'Do we receive anything to say that we have graduated?' asks Brian.

(Applause)

He is smiling broadly like he is indicating that his question is a light-hearted one.

'What did you want?' asks Kim. 'A certificate that says, I am not an arsehole?'

(Laughter)

There is more sharing and finally, as before, the remainder of the session is taken up with logistics. We are informed that the final weekend sessions will take place at a different location from the hotel, namely, Queens Studios in Salusbury Road, North West London. We are provided with details for getting to and from the venue. Once again, I agree to drop off Jed and Marjory this evening and pick them up on Saturday morning.

We emerge from the hotel at Ten Thirty.

Second Saturday

We are gathered in the entrance of Queens Studios, the Programmes Ltd. head office, on Salusbury Road which is a short walk from Queens Park underground station. It is a nice old Victorian building with a wide entrance that leads from the street through to a courtyard that backs on to Paddington Old Cemetery. We go upstairs and enter a bright and airy space that is like a large studio room. A hand rail runs along half the length of the room. It is the type of rail that you might see in a ballet class. In front of the hand rail stands a tall stool with some notes resting on the seat.

We are ushered in by a couple of friendly trainers. I find that I am still slightly surprised that they have not resumed their stony faced demeanour. They tell us that we can leave our coats and bags in the small lobby area at the entrance to the studio. We are not relieved of our watches. Although everyone enters the room and communicates with one another in an energised manner the mood seems to be one of relaxed expectation. We sit on ergonomically designed kneeling chairs which are laid out in seven long rows of around twenty chairs per row.

After a few minutes Kim enters the room. Once again, she is dressed in a blue business suit with a crisp white blouse. On reflection, I suppose that you might call her mode of dress, power dressing.

We get going with some sharing on the week's events. It is interesting that some people seem more enthusiastic and ready to share than some of the others. In fact there are one or two trainees that I don't remember having shared at all. Clearly, Kim is aware of this and challenges the *energy burglars*, as she refers to the non sharers, to, 'come out from behind the curtain'.

'You know who you are,' she says. 'You're like black holes sucking all the energy out of the room.'

'I've been hiding,' says Sandy.

Sandy is slight and pale. She looks to be in her late twenties or early thirties. She is wearing an ankle length skirt that is thin and almost see-through. On top she wears a copper brown cardigan that is too big for her, over a white t-shirt.

'I've been frightened to stand up in public. When we were doing the cathartic experience process last Sunday I chose my fear of speaking. I remembered a specific incidence where I felt fear. I was afraid of looking foolish in front of my parents. I was made to learn some school work by rote and I couldn't get it right. It turned out that I wasn't afraid of speaking in public. I was afraid that I wouldn't get approval from my parents.'

(Applause)

'I want to share that I have been more energised than I have ever been. I have got more done at work and everyone notices the difference in me,' says Joe. 'People have asked me what had happened. I didn't tell anyone. I just said that I was feeling good. The only person who didn't notice was my boss. He was the same old same old. No recognition or acknowledgement.'

'He noticed alright,' says Kim. 'He's shitting himself even more now.'

(Laughter and applause for Joe)

'I thought that I hadn't really understood what was going on last

150

week,' says Mike.

Mike is a man who is, I would guess, in his early forties. He has thinning hair and wears a white shirt and trousers from an old suit.

'In fact, let me put it straight, I didn't understand what was going on last week.'

(Laughter)

'I got home early on Monday morning and went to bed. I got up a few hours later and carried on as normal, all week. Friday, a colleague at work asks me if I've got a new car. I look at him bewildered. He says that I have got to work early every day for the first time he can remember. How about that?'

(Laughter and applause)

'My girlfriend told me that a friend of hers got mugged the other night,' says Pat. 'I was trying to explain about responsibility and how, if you take responsibility, your choices become better and you're less likely to get mugged. But she didn't get it. She asked me to explain how our choices could affect what we didn't know was going to happen. I didn't know what to say. I know I have to take responsibility for not getting my point across better.'

'I know a little story about something like that,' says Kim. 'A Monk is telling a student about taking responsibility and the student asks him how can he take responsibility for unforeseen circumstances?

"What if you are standing on a precipice and there is a tiger coming to attack you. There is no way you can get past the tiger to escape. You can't climb down because the tiger's mate is waiting below. What would you do? How would taking responsibility help you if that happened?"

And the Monk replies,

"It is simple. I wouldn't get myself into such a foolish situation

151

in the first place." You see?' Kim asks.

Pat nods his head.

Kim smiles and continues.

'When you assume complete responsibility, your decisions become sharper, your cognitive processes and judgements become keener, your actions become stronger. It is almost as if you have turned on a luck switch. It feels like everything has started to go your way.'

(Applause for Pat)

The sharing goes on for perhaps another forty minutes. Everyone is clearly more relaxed than last week. The mood is light and some of the trainees actually look like they are enjoying it.

'Before we go on I want to explore an area that is going to be vital to you once you have completed the seminar.'

Kim is standing at the front of the long rows of kneeling seats. She walks slowly up and down as she speaks. I notice that she picks out people and seems to direct what she is saying to them individually before moving on to someone else. It occurs to me that Robert does the same thing.

'By tomorrow you will all have got it. Which, for some of you, will be whether you like it or not.'

(Laughter)

'So I want to address something that will come up after you have completed the seminar. I want to explore what we know about communication. After all, we don't want you charging out of here like a herd of enlightened buffalos stampeding over everyone with your new found personal power.'

(Laughter)

'You are going to have to communicate. So what is communication? What makes up an act of communication?'

Kim invites us to provide some ideas. We offer suggestions like:

Talking

Sharing ideas

Exchanging information

'The dictionary definition is: transmission, to impart, to give or exchange messages or information, to be connected with,' she continues. 'All of these items are essential for communication. If one of them is missing there is no communication. There is, however one component that sticks out as often being missing but not noticed. That is: *being connected.* I mean, if there is no giving or exchanging of messages or information then obviously there is no communication. But, you can have all of these and not be *connected* so it may appear as if you are communicating but you are not. If you are going to take responsibility for communicating then you must connect.'

For me, this section of the seminar feels like a training guide for those who might go on to work for Programmes. I am impatient to move on to the *getting it* bit, although I know that this comes tomorrow, on the Sunday. I am sure a few others feel the same way.

'You know what it is like,' Kim continues. 'You go into a bank and there's the person behind the glass window, looking down, not looking at you. You hand over your cheque or whatever and they hand over your money, still not looking at you. I feel like rapping on the glass with my knuckles and saying, SHALL WE CONNECT.'

Kim points her forefinger. She moves it back and forth as if she is pointing first to the imaginary bank clerk's eye and then her own.

'Let's get some communication going shall we? Some eye contact,' she continues.

(Laughter)

'So we are going to do a process. I want you to stand up, select a person and connect with them, without touching. Introduce yourself and tell them, what you are experiencing, tell them an idea, or say something about someone in the room. When the other person feels they have got what you're saying they acknowledge you. So for example, you may say, "My name is Kim. I am angry that Steve keeps falling asleep in the room." OK?'

(Laughter)

'The other person then says, "I get that you're angry." Don't forget, *nothing going on*, as you say it. And remember to breath.'

We go through the process. Personally, I find it difficult to come up with an experience other than apathy. I haven't really got anything to say about anyone in the room and I am short on ideas right now.

'Hi, my name is Arthur and I am experiencing apathy around this process.'

I look into Mani's eyes and try to *connect*.

'I *get* that you feel apathy,' she says after thirty seconds or so.

'Hello, my name is Sam. I am really enjoying today compared with last week.'

We lock our eyes for thirty seconds.

'I *get* that you are enjoying today,' I say.

After an hour has passed I find that I am really struggling. I suspect that I am not the only one who is not into this process or indeed this part of the seminar. This is confirmed when Kim chastises Carl for looking at his watch.

'If you keep checking the time Carl I'm going to take that watch off of you.'

Kim walks over to Carl and leans forward to *connect* with him.

154

'Do you get that I am angry?' she says.

'I get that you are angry,' says Carl.

His voice is timid.

'And we all *get* that Carl is *getting* fear,' I think to myself. 'Fear of Kim.'

A half an hour later Kim calls a halt to the process.

'We refer to this form of connected communication as *controlled aggression*,' she says. 'OK, let's have some sharing on what you got around that process.'

'I felt that it was a very powerful means of communication,' says Pat. 'You can really see if the other person has got what you are communicating.'

(Applause)

'It's good but it will only work if the other person wants to be connected,' says James.

(Applause)

'You must engage with the person,' says Kim. 'Don't start to communicate until you are connected. If you have to say, "shall we connect," then so be it. But, I can assure you, if you search for a connection through eye contact then you will establish that connection. If not they'll probably run away.'

(Laughter)

'Which doesn't matter as you wouldn't be able to communicate with them anyway.'

'One of the things I have really got from this seminar is eye contact,' says Tania. 'Like I said last week, I had always avoided making eye contact. I suppose it was a confidence thing. All of the way through we have been learning to make this connection. I think it is great. I can see that this alone will help me in my life. I can't wait to try it out.

Outside I mean.'

(Applause)

There is forty minutes more of sharing around *controlled aggression*. I find it surprising how many people think positively about the idea and embrace it. Perhaps I am being overly dismissive around the idea.

At one forty five Kim calls a break for one hour, which is longer than last week's first breaks. I go to a cafe on Salusbury Road with Jed and Brian. I say that the last session felt a bit like a pre Programmes sales training course.

'It'll be useful though,' says Brian.

'I didn't mind it,' says Jed.

'Either of you two thinking of working for Programmes after this?' I ask.

'Nah!' says Brian.

'Don't think so,' says Jed.

We return to Queens Studios. A few people are walking along Salusbury Road smoking on the way back. This is because Kim had asked the smokers to refrain from smoking outside the building, in the courtyard area.

Back inside the studio room we take our seats.

'There is no need to avoid sitting next to a person that you know or who you have sat next to before,' says Kim. 'You are past that now. You can have that prop back next time.'

(Laughter)

'Next, we are going to take a look at our parents,' she continues.

There are a few groans from the trainees.

'I can tell that this is going to be very helpful for some of you,' she says.

(Laughter)

'I am going to ask you some questions and I want you to write down the answers in your notebooks.'

We take out our notebooks and pencils.

'Write down how your parents relate to one and other.'

Kim waits for a few moments while we scribble down our notes.

'How are your relationships like your parents' relationships?'

'In what ways are you like your parents?'

'What percentage are you, mother to father? For example: are you sixty percent father, forty percent mother, thirty percent father seventy percent mother?'

Kim waits until we have finished writing.

'Anyone want to get going with the sharing?' she asks. 'Yes Laura. Tell us first how your parents relate or related to one and other.'

'Well,' says Laura.

Laura has her notebook open. She is not reading from it but using what she has written as a prompt.

'My parents, they always struck me that they were a team but, as I've got older, I think that my father was really in charge in a lot of ways. I mean, they discuss things but my mother always acquiesces to my father's wishes. They are happy though. Well, I assume they're happy. I've never asked.'

Laura stops and laughs.

'Maybe I will after this.'

157

(Laughter)

'In what way are you like your parents?'

'I suppose I am like my mother in that I'm very passive, you know. People say I look like my aunt, my father's sister. So I might take after his side of the family physically.'

Laura looks down at her hands.

'I've got my mother's hands though,' she says and wiggles her fingers.

'And what about relationships? Do you tend to acquiesce to your partner in your relationships?' Kim asks.

'I do, I suppose. Although I haven't had to make any big decisions with my partner, I generally let him make the decisions.'

'So, in your relationships, would you say you were more like your mother?'

'I am,' says Laura. 'But in other ways I am more like my father. I like things done in a certain way like he does.'

'Such as?'

'Oh, how the flat is decorated, what furniture we have. What we eat. That sort of thing.'

'How do you get your partner to agree to have these things the way that you want them?'

'I can get a bit of a strop on occasionally if I don't get my way.'

Laura laughs.

'Then he suggests that you both do it the way you want it and you acquiesce?'

'Yes, more or less.'

'Are you sure that isn't what your mother does with your father and in fact it is she who is getting her way.'

'Now I think about it, yes.'

158

'What did you write down about what percentage are you. Mother to father?'

'I wrote: sixty five percent father and thirty five percent mother. But now I think I've got those the wrong way round.'

Laura laughs. She looks quite shocked at the revelation.

(Laughter)

'You may be surprised by it,' says Kim. 'But, I imagine, it s more to do with the fact that you never thought about your parents' relationship. Thank you Laura.'

(Applause)

'It is easy to see our parents as just *our parents* and not as people. We have to remind ourselves that they are people too. With the same rackets and hang ups, the same propensity for beliefs and all of the rest of the shit, that we have,' says Kim. 'Parents are people too you know.'

(Laughter)

Kim walks along the front row of trainees.

'It is interesting how some people exercise control in relationships. Laura does the same thing as her mother. She controls the situation by her moods. It's a given that she learnt that from her mother without even realizing it. Can anyone give me some other examples of control?'

'My parents were always rowing. My old man was a drunk,' says Kay. 'He used to come in after he'd been to the pub and there'd be a shouting match. He used to give my mum a slap but she'd hit him back twice as hard. I'm like my mother. I wouldn't want to be like him.'

'Did your father always drink?'

'Ever since I can remember.'

'Your mother must have seen something in him.'

'He knocked my mum up with me. Said he did the right thing by marrying her but spent his life regretting it. Talk about not taking responsibility, the prick.'

(Laughter)

'How are you like them?'

'Well I don't get pissed up all the time like him, that's for sure.'

(Laughter)

'I am strong, like my mum. But at the same time I'm wary of men. Not surprising really. Occasionally though, if we are arguing, she says that I am just like my father.'

'Have you ever asked her in which way she thinks you are like him?'

'Sarcastic. She says I can be sarcastic like he was. I remember, when I was young, he did like a laugh. But that all stopped when the drinking increased. It was funny. He died a couple of years ago. I still felt sad when he went like. Me mum misses him I know. Even if she won't admit it.'

'Do you think your mother got pregnant on purpose to get your father to marry her?' Kim asks.

'Probably,' says Kay. 'She can be a bit manipulative, you know. I suppose I can be too. A controlling bastard I mean.'

Kay laughs and starts to sit.

'And just for the record, I get grief when I think about it or talk about it,' she says.

Kay sits. The trace of a tear trickles down her cheek. She leaves it to trickle. There is loud applause for her.

'Kay is probably the most naturally *in touch* person in the room,' says Kim.

'Yes, Paul.'

'My father died a couple of years ago. But I think my parents had a good relationship. They always seemed happy,' he says.

'How are you like them?'

'Well, I'm generally a happy person too.'

'And are you happy in your relationships?' asks Kim.

'I haven't got a girlfriend at the moment.'

'Boyfriend?' asks Kim.

(Laughter)

'No,' says Paul.

He is laughing but a little red in the face.

'Friends then?' asks Kim. 'Boys or girls. You don't have to be fucking them to have a relationship you know.'

(Laughter)

'Yes, I am happy around my friends.'

'And who would you say you are more like, father or mother?'

'I always thought my father but after Laura I'm not sure,' he says.

(Laughter)

'And in terms of percentages?' asks Kim.

'I would say I'm fifty fifty. An equal amount of both.'

'Yeh! Pretty bland,' says Kim.

(Applause)

The sharing goes on for another forty five minutes or so. It is oddly fascinating to hear about other people parents and their situations. Kim highlights various aspects of our parents' relationships and the similarities in our own behaviour.

'I just want to share that I find it really interesting how we seem

161

to pick up our parents' traits and make them into our own,' says Mac.

'That's how you acquire most of your rackets,' says Kim. 'And for those among us who are approval seeking arseholes like Mac.'

(Laughter)

'Much of that racket has come from your parents as well. That need to be pleasant all the time, no matter how false, is partly the need to get approval from mummy and daddy. We'll be exploring other areas of approval seeking behaviour tomorrow.'

Kim is leaning slightly against the wall with the hand rail. She has her arms stretched out and her hands resting on the rail.

'You seek approval from your friends. You are worried about what people think about you. You are scared of criticism. Much of it goes back to your parents.'

She pushes herself away from the rail and walks towards the first row of chairs.

'For those of you that can't say no, for example. You can't say no because you don't want to upset anyone. Mummy and daddy approval. This doesn't mean that you can blame your parents though. You created your approval seeking behaviour. You have to take responsibility for it.'

Kim stands and looks to see if any more hands are going up.

'Ok, let's move on,' she says

Kim then asks us to write down fifteen things about ourselves.

'I want you to write down the question and then the answer. Don't spend too long on trying to come up with your answer or your beliefs will get in the way. And don't hold back on the truth. I am not going to get you read them out.'

(Laughter)

The questions are:

Are you emotional?

162

Can you dance?

Have you constantly been told something throughout your life?

What are you most afraid of?

What is the hardest thing to do when relating to others?

What are you not worthy of?

What is your biggest concern?

What is your biggest fear around sex?

What gives you grief?

What can't you get enough of?

What can't you forgive yourself for?

When are you most helpless?

When do you feel inadequate?

What do you wish?

When do you get ill?

I am surprised at how easily the answers flow. As soon as I write the question the answer pops into my head. Sometimes I don't like the answers but there is no kidding yourself now.

'OK. Now I want you write down the things you like about yourself. Write: what I like about myself is. Then, underneath, write the answers.'

Kim waits while we scribble.

'Now, things that you don't like about yourself.'

Kim waits again.

'Next write what you like and don't like about your father and your mother.'

It is odd how this becomes a sort of truth process. I look around and everyone is scribbling intently. It seems to be having the same effect on everyone else.

163

'Now what you like and don't like about your lover, or ex lover. Or ex *lovers* in your case Snick.'

(Laughter)

'Now I want you to write down what gives you pleasure.'

Again, Kim waits for us to finish writing.

'And now, your fears.'

We continue to write out our responses.

'Is this session designed to help us become more aware of our own personality traits and where they have come from?' asks Snick.

'That is exactly what it is designed to do,' Kim replies. 'I had no idea you were cerebral.'

(Laughter and applause for Snick)

We finish writing.

'Next,' says Kim, 'we are going to identify something that you all have. It is something that stops you from getting *satisfaction*. It is what we call an *unwanted, continued, persistent, experience.*'

Kim walks to the end of the first row of trainees and repeats her last phrase.

'An unwanted, continued, persistent, experience. I want you to write this down:

What I want is....

What I get is....

So

What I really want is....

Because I am scared of....

Fill in what is pertinent to you. For example, it might be: What I want is a good relationship. What I get is a bad relationship. So, what I really want is a bad relationship. Because, I am scared of commitment.'

We scribble down the phrases and once again I am surprised at how the answer to what I am scared of pops into my head.

'Being scared you tend to avoid the things that you are scared of. Write down what you are scared of. Write down your beliefs around these things.'

Once again we fill our note books with these ponderings.

'OK. Let's share a few of these.' says Kim.

'Here we go,' says Matt.

He takes a deep breath.

'What I want is money. What I get is poverty. So, what I really want is poverty because I am frightened of failing.'

'Very good Matt,' says Kim. 'Your fear of failure is responsible for your unwanted, continued, persistent, experience. Can you identify what the drama of the situation is?'

'Yes. When I wrote down the question: have you constantly been told something throughout your life? I immediately put: to be careful, not to fail. You see my parents always thought I should get a steady job and income but I wanted to do photography. I didn't do what I wanted to do. That's why I have been sort of drifting. You know, in the employment sense. That's why I don't have any money.'

'OK,' says Kim. 'First off, you chose not to get into photography. Your choice.'

'Yes,' says Matt.

He nods his head in acceptance.

'So, the drama is that your parents had been telling you not to take any risks and to get a steady job. You experienced fear. Fear that you might fail if you followed your ambition. Then your parents would be right. The reality of it is: that you get fear. And you have been going around all this time avoiding your experience of fear, hiding behind your

165

rackets. So get in touch with that fear. Be afraid. Explore it. And give up wanting to change it.'

Matt is nodding his head vigorously.

'Yes,' he says. 'I *get* it.'

(Applause)

'Who's next?'

'What I want is my own place to live but what I get is living with my parents. So what I want is to live with my parents because I am afraid of being on my own,' says Karen.

When I first saw Karen she looked like she could be in her forties. I now realize that she is in her early thirties. She has looked progressively younger as the seminar has gone on.

'Why don't you live with someone other than you parents?' Kim asks.

'I don't really know anyone that I think I could live with.'

'And that's why you choose to live with your parents.'

'I don't really want to live on my own but I don't want to be living with my parents all of my life. I had a fiancée but that didn't work out. I haven't found anybody since.'

'Do you have more than one fear around living on your own?'

'I suppose I am frightened of intimacy. Of being in an environment with someone I don't know.'

'You know what to do now don't you Karen,' says Kim.

Kim is being almost gentle with Karen in her speech and demeanour. It is a side of Kim's nature that has not been overly evident up until now.

'Get in touch with my fears, experience them and give up wanting to change them.'

Kim nods her head.

166

'Thank you Karen.'

(Applause)

The trainees share in a similar way to Matt and Karen. Kim re-iterates that it is avoiding our experience that holds us back and the experience we usually get is fear. She reminds us constantly that we must give up trying to change our experience.

Around twenty people have shared what they have written. The sharing goes on for about two hours.

Eventually, Kim says that we can take a break for one and a half hours. We stream out. It is five forty five in the afternoon. Strangely, I am not surprised that everyone seems to be able to cope with the long sessions much easier this weekend. Although I have been hungry for a couple of hours it seems less of an issue this week.

I have some dinner with Jed and Brian. We are joined by Marjory, Greg and Fran. We discuss the day's proceedings. I say that for me, today has been the least enjoyable or interesting day of the entire seminar. Brian and Jed agree. Fran says that, for her, today has been a revelation.

'I had no idea I was so like my mother,' she says. 'I had always thought I was more like my father. I guess that was how I wanted to see myself.'

Fran thinks for a moment and continues.

'Do you three think that today has been the least enjoyable day because you are avoiding your experience around your parents?' she asks.

Brian, Jed and I laugh.

'Probably,' says Jed.

Marjory says that, although she enjoyed today and thought it worthwhile, she can't wait for tomorrow.

'When Kuh Kim was talking about seeking approval, she cuh could have been talking about me,' says Greg. 'It's no wonder I stutter all the time.'

Greg laughs when he realizes that he just completed the last sentence without stuttering.

'Fuh Fucking amazing,' he says mimicking himself.

We return to the studio room and take our seats. Everyone appears to be very relaxed, almost serene. Kim enters.

'Has everybody got where we are at this moment?' she asks. 'Let's have some more people sharing on unwanted, continued, persistent experiences.'

'What I want is my relationship to work, what I get is my relationship not working, so, what I want is my relationship not to work because I am afraid of being tied to someone that I feel I've made a mistake with.'

It is Cally, the Canadian lady.

'Why are you afraid of being tied to someone if you've made a mistake? It is simple. Leave,' says Kim.

'Because I feel that I should try to make it work. I chose to get involved.'

'I don't understand,' says Kim. 'Are you sure that your experience is fear? Come on. What are you getting when you choose to have your relationship how it is?'

Cally thinks for a few moments.

'Actually I'm angry,' she says. 'I'm angry with myself for

getting myself in this situation. The relationship made it easier for me to stay in the country. I thought I could make my partner fit in with what I wanted. Be how I wanted him to be. I tried to take an easy route and it hasn't worked and I'm angry.'

'You can't change people,' says Kim. 'Love is the ability to allow someone to exist in your space, unchanged, with all their quirks and behavioural traits intact.'

'Yes,' says Cally. 'That is exactly it. Deep down, on an almost instinctive level, I knew that. I am angry with myself for getting involved with someone and then trying to change them.'

Cally lets out a long sigh, takes a deep breath and stands really straight.

'I know what to do now though,' she says.

(Applause)

The sharing continues for another hour and a half before Kim draws the session to a close. Once again, she ensures that everyone can get home and make it back in tomorrow.

Just before we are about to leave Mac puts his hand up and asks a question.

'I want to ask about getting it.'

There are groans from the trainees.

'Come on then,' says Kim.

'I know that the only thing that I can rely on as being real is my experience,' says Mac. 'I know that what I perceive is filtered through the beliefs that I have accumulated, giving rise to my experience, my emotion. I know that by not trying to change the emotion, by just experiencing it, the emotion can be transformed. But what I want to know is have I *got* it and if not how will I know when I do *get* it?'

'You will know,' says Kim. 'And that will come tomorrow. In the meantime I want you all to acknowledge that you are willing to let go of wanting to change your experience. That you are willing to be with your experience.'

Some people nod their heads.

(Applause for Mac)

'OK, you can go,' says Kim. 'I recommend that you arrive well rested. Tomorrow is the day,' she says.

It is ten thirty, another positively early finish.

Second Sunday

There are plenty of parking spaces near Queens Studios today. I am with Jed and Marjory and we are walking along Salusbury Road.

'Are you excited?' asks Jed.

'Yes,' I reply.

'This could be the day when all of our dreams come true,' says Marjory.

We arrive at Queens Studios. Once again there are just two trainers present. We pick up our name tags, leave our bags and coats and take our seats. The room is the same as the day before. At the front is the tall stool with some papers on top of it. Kim enters. She is dressed, as usual, in a smart business suit with a crisp white blouse. She picks up the papers from the stool.

'Let's start with some sharing,' she says. 'About yesterday's proceedings or whatever you wish.'

'I want to share that I have been really looking forward to today,' says Kate. 'I've felt so good since last week I'm fascinated to see if I can feel any better.'

'It's all right to look forward,' says Kim. 'But don't forget, your experience is in the here and now. Well, the near past anyway. It is getting in touch with your experience and taking responsibility that are the keys to ensuring the continuity of your feeling of wellbeing. That and what you will get later today.'

(Applause for Kate)

'I finally explained about responsibility to my girlfriend last night and she got it,' says Pat. 'I used the controlled aggression communication and the examples that you gave. She is going to do the next seminar.'

(Applause)

'I just want to say that I am starting to get in touch with what I am experiencing and it is provoking a change in the way in which I view other people,' says Simon.

Simon has not retained his leather elbow patch, pipe smokers' jacket. He has opted for corduroy trousers and a pullover today.

People share how they feel, what they thought of the previous day's sessions and other issues that seem important to them but might not necessarily appear so to the rest of the trainees. The mood is what you might call forgiving. Nobody appears to be irritated or impatient as might have been the case last weekend.

After around half an hour Kim calls a halt to the sharing. She walks up and down in front of the first row of trainees. She waives away a couple of hands that are raised. It is as if she is collecting her thoughts.

'We are going to talk a little about our rational mind,' she says. 'We touched on some aspects of it throughout the seminar. If you remember, those of you who have managed to stay awake.'

(Laughter)

'So let's have a look at what the rational mind is. What is it? What is its purpose? Anyone got any ideas?'

'Ego,' offers Dan.

'The rational mind isn't the ego nor is the ego the purpose of the rational mind,' says Kim.

(Applause)

'Logic,' says Sam. 'It allows us to think logically, to work things out.'

'OK,' says Kim.

(Applause)

'It's our intellect, thought, awareness. It enables us to conceptualise. To make judgements,' says Marjory.

'Very good,' says Kim.

(Applause for Marjory)

'So what is it?' asks Kim.

'It's the brain, the self, the being,' says Mac

Kim nods her head as if she is agreeing with him.

(Applause)

'Sanity,' says Carol. 'Without a rational mind and intellect we couldn't behave in a sane way. People would act irrationally.'

'Would you say that the rational mind is essential then?' asks Kim.

'Of course it is essential. It allows us to operate in the world,' says Carol. 'We couldn't live without it.'

(Applause for Carol)

'So what is the purpose of the rational mind?'

'Does it have to have a purpose?' asks James. 'Perhaps it just *is*.'

'No, it has a purpose James, a very definite purpose.'

(Applause)

'To store information that allows us to make decisions,' offers Chas.

(Applause)

'That is part of its function,' says Kim. 'The storing of

information isn't its purpose though.'

'Like Carol said, it allows us to operate in the world, to survive,' says Jerry.

'It allows us to operate in the world, to survive,' Kim repeats Jerry's answer.

(Applause for Jerry)

Kim pauses for a few seconds.

'The purpose of the rational mind is survival. We have evolved as creatures with a rational mind but our basic instincts remain unchanged. Number one, survive, number two, procreate. Without survival there can be no procreation so the rational mind's primary objective is survival.'

Kim pauses for a few seconds.

'And would you say that the rational mind would regard itself as being in control of the whole being?'

'Yes,' says Carol. 'The brain or the mind if you like, has to be in charge of the being.'

'Thank you Carol,' says Kim.

(Applause)

'You see,' Kim continues, 'the rational mind works from the premise that it is the whole being and that, as part of the survival of the being, it is essential that the rational mind survives. The rational mind is concerned with its own survival. It is important to understand that the rational mind regards the being as anything that it identifies itself with or considers itself to be. The human mind's notion of survival extends beyond the survival of the body. That is why, in some circumstances, the mind will rationalise a course of action that puts the survival of the body, or the being, at risk of death. Why, for example, would someone run into a burning building to save a child if the purpose of the rational mind is the survival of the being? It is because, for that person, the rational mind's idea of itself encapsulates the notion that the survival of the child is necessary to the survival of the being.'

'Would you say that is why some people do seemingly irrational things like young men fighting at football matches and so forth?' asks Simon.

'It is,' replies Kim. 'In this case the young man might consider it to be important to show himself as strong, masculine and brave. He identifies not with his body but his conception of how he should be. So when he ends up outside a football ground fighting and getting stabbed his mind is still working for the survival of what it identifies as the being.'

'Yes I understand. You could, then, say that the same thing is happening with people who choose to be martyrs,' adds Simon. 'Their rational mind sees the whole being as a devout, godly person whose ultimate survival might depend on an act that leads to death. They may see death as a part of the route to ultimate survival.'

Kim nods her head.

(Applause for Simon)

'What about suicide though,' says Snick. 'Martyrdom is not strictly suicide, is it? It might get you killed but you're not killing yourself are you? How can people commit suicide if the rational mind's basic instinct is to survive? How can the mind rationalise that?'

'It is the same thing,' replies Kim. 'There can be a number of explanations. Don't forget the rational mind's concept of survival extends beyond the body, even though that notion of survival might kill the body. For example, someone may have a belief that says there is an afterlife and that we have a soul and a spirit. In a given situation their rational mind might reason that the only way that the soul and spirit can survive is in the afterlife. So suicide seems a way of ensuring our survival.'

'Crazy,' says Snick.

'That is how crazy the rational mind and beliefs can seem. It is incredible really, the things us arseholes conjure up.'

(Laughter and applause for Snick)

It is the first time that I have heard either Kim or Robert refer to themselves as arseholes.

Kim, once again, walks to the end of the first row of trainees.

'We are going to do a process,' she says. 'We are going to listen to the voice of our reason, our *internal dialogue*. That little voice in your head chattering away all of the time. It is this dialogue that upholds our view of the world. We can't stop it. We can't help but do it. We talk to ourselves all of the time. It is our rational mind keeping up a flow of dialogue, keeping itself at the forefront of our being, staying in charge. I want you to become aware of it. Find a quiet space in the room, on your own and sit quietly with your eyes closed for a few minutes and listen to it. When I say go I want you to write down, in your notebooks, what comes up. It doesn't matter what. Just write it down.'

We spread out to the sides of the room and sit quietly and listen to the flow of thoughts that tumble across our minds. When directed we write them down.

'OK, back to your seats.'

We return to our seats.

'Now we're going to read them out.'

(Groans)

'Who wants to be first?'

Celia raises her hand then stands and starts to read.

'Sunshine through the window, I can feel the warmth, carpet smells nice, hungry, missed breakfast, bloody bus, oops, don't blame.'

(Laughter)

'Traffic noise, hadn't noticed it before, birdsong too, springtime, a sneeze. That was all,' she says.

(Applause)

'Yes Carl.'

'This is bollocks,' he starts.

(Laughter)

'Hate this process, what's going on, quiet, has everyone left, ha ha, open my eyes, no, wait, shit, ready, forgotten what I'm doing, breathe, tired, wake up.'

'Thank you Carl,' says Kim.

(Applause)

More of us share what we have written. It is slightly unnerving speaking out loud ones inner thoughts, however trivial or meaningless, it feels odd to lay bear our private thoughts.

'Snick. You're next,' says Kim. 'I can see you trying to hide over there. I can smell you wanting to avoid sharing what you've written. I've sniffed you out. Up you get.'

(Laughter)

Snick stands smiling and reads.

'Fuck, tired, I fancy Kim.'

(Laughter)

'Bet all the blokes do, hope this doesn't get read out.'

(Laughter)

'Shit, hate those poncey chairs,'

177

(Laughter)

'fuck, get car fixed, next week, tired. That's all,' he says.

Snick sits. He looks sheepishly apologetic.

'Thank you,' says Kim.

She is completely unfazed by the comments.

(Applause for Snick)

After a few more readings Kim continues.

'This voice is our rational mind telling us that the world is how we chose it to be, that it is such and such and so and so. It upholds our beliefs. It re-enforces the rational mind's concept of the being, of itself. We wanted you to get in touch with it. You'll see why later.'

Kim calls a break. She advises us to get something to eat as the next session will be a long one.

'Don't stuff your faces though,' she says. 'You need to be alert because when you get back. It will be time for you to *get* it.'

We leave the room. It is one thirty. I am with Jed, Brian, Marjory, Greg and Fran. The six of us walk along Salusbury Road. Most of the shops are closed for the Sunday. Further along we find a little place that does pizzas.

'Perfect for a pre-enlightenment brunch,' says Marjory.

'I'm so excited I can hardly eat,' says Fran.

We return from our break and are seated in the room. Robert enters. There is resounding applause as he walks to the centre of the studio room. As usual he is dressed immaculately in a dark suit and a shirt and tie. The sense of anticipation is tangible, like an aroma.

178

'I am going to get straight on with it so pay attention,' says Robert.

A number of the trainees shift in their seats.

'This morning we looked at the purpose of the rational mind. Which is?' he asks.

'Survival,' says Marjory.

(Applause for Marjory)

'We can cut out the acknowledgement now,' says Robert. 'There's no need to clap. We're past that and you've almost *got it.*'

A few of the trainees look surprised. I am happy and relieved not to be clapping all the time.

'Yes survival,' continues Robert. 'And we have seen that the rational mind's concept of itself is not only the being but anything that it considers itself to be and consequently its survival extends beyond the survival of the entire being. To *get it* we need to understand how we work. We need to be clear on what makes us tick. What makes up our rational mind? How does the rational mind function? How do we get our beliefs? Why do we choose certain experiences, certain emotions? Why do some people get angry at something and others don't? Why do some people get joy around something and other don't?'

Robert is standing in the middle and in front of the first long row of kneeling chairs. He is picking out individuals in the crowd with his eyes and directing what he is saying to them. It is as if he is speaking to you and you alone.

'So, how does the rational mind function?'

Robert pauses for a few moments.

'For the sake of explanation we have created a character that represents our rational mind, our reason. We call this character Rat.'

Robert makes a facial gesture that is just like a rat. He raises his

179

hands to his face and moves them as if he is preening his whiskers with his paws.

(Laughter)

'Rat is very clever,' he continues. 'He takes everything in. Every bit of information that comes through your senses, Rat processes it, records it, and logs it.'

Robert holds his left hand to his eye and makes an aperture like a camera lens. With his right hand he turns an imaginary crank so he mimics a silent film camera being hand cranked.

(Laughter)

'He can record sound too,' he says. 'And touch and smell and taste.'

Robert cups his hand to his ear like he is straining to listen. He makes a gesture like he has touched something hot. He then acts like he has a bad smell under his nose and finally smacks his lips like he has an odd taste in his mouth.

(Laughter)

'Rat observes, takes in, records and stores vast amounts of multi sensory information. He stores this information in files. There is a lot of data and therefore a lot of files. All stored away in the brain's filing cabinets.'

Robert turns and does an impression of somebody opening a filing cabinet and placing a file in to it.

'The rational mind,' he says. 'And herein lies the problem for us humans. Because of this rational mind we have something that no other creature has and that is the ego.'

Robert pauses for a few seconds.

'Forget what you've read about the ego. Hindus and Buddhists and Psychologists and Psychiatrists have been batting on about the ego for years. Put simply, the ego is what we call the situation when the entire being, mind and body, associates itself as the rational mind. When the rational mind, or good old Rat as we are calling him, with his filing cabinets and information and files assumes the role of existing as the whole being we get ego. When, as is inevitable in humans, the rational mind identifies itself and sees itself as the whole being we get ego.'

Again Robert pauses. He has been scrutinising the trainees as if to satisfy himself that we are all keeping up. There is no problem. When I look around, the trainees are on the edge of their seats. The concentration levels in the room are extremely high.

'So what is the purpose of the rational mind?' he asks.

'Survival,' says Brian.

'Of what?' asks Robert.

'The being,' replies Brian.

'And what does the rational mind regard as being *the being*?'

'Itself.'

'Yes, very good Brian.' says Robert. 'The purpose of Rat, the rational mind is survival and this, consequently, means its own survival. Its purpose becomes the survival of the mind and the survival of the mind means the survival of the files, the viewpoints, the thoughts, the conclusions and the beliefs that are all contained in the files that are stored in the filing cabinets.'

Robert is slowly pacing up and down in front of us.

'And the rational mind acts to ensure its survival by constantly trying to find a place to fit new information into a file that it already has. It acts to ensure its survival by constantly trying to prove itself right. Rat is always seeking affirmation of itself. It constantly needs to justify itself and it will do anything to achieve what it considers pertinent to ensure survival. So if the mind needs to sustain itself as it is and it requires

181

justification of itself, what do you think it looks for?'

'Minds that think the same way,' says Cally.

'Yes, minds that think the same. What is another word for it?'

'Affirmation,' someone says.

'Yes affirmation,' says Robert.

'Conformity or similarity,' says someone else.

'Agreement,' says Jed.

'Yes agreement,' says Robert. 'The mind has to be right. It has to prove itself right and to do so it seeks agreement which provides approval for itself.'

Robert sweeps over the trainees with his eyes. His face shows a wry smile.

'I bet more than half of you finally chose to attend the seminar because you convinced yourselves that Exegesis sounded just like the sort of thing you had been looking for all along.'

There is some self conscious laughter from those of us that this applies to.

'People choose to become involved with things that affirm what they already believe,' Robert continues. 'They read the books that re-affirm their beliefs, they are drawn to religions that re-affirm their beliefs. People and their rational minds choose things that they are comfortable with and reject that which they are not comfortable with. That's why your Rat constantly tried to put you to sleep throughout this seminar. We have not been telling you what your reason, your rational mind, your Rat, wants to hear. Even now your Rat is trying to put what I'm saying into an old file.'

Robert does his rat impression and strokes his chin like he is deep in thought.

'Hmm! Now I've got it, the mind is like a filing cabinet.'

(Laughter)

'All that means is that Rat has found a place in its belief system that accommodates what we've been saying. Rat only wants to understand what is already filed away,' he continues. 'Rat has to consistently prove himself right to survive. He constantly needs to utilise and re-utilise the existing information contained in the files. The files and the filing system must survive. Rat is like a tape recording on a continuous loop playing back the information contained in the files. Remember the cheese and the five boxes? Rat doesn't want any cheese. He wants to keep playing the survival tape of opening the fifth box.'

(Some laughter)

'Remember the session with the unwanted, continued, persistent experience? We don't get any cheese because we don't want any cheese. We just want to keep opening the fifth box.'

(More laughter)

'OK. So let's have a closer look at how our Rats function. We'll try and see how this evolved.'

Once again Robert does a masterful impression of a rat.

'To make this simple,' he continues, 'let's pick a simple basic human. Let's imagine a stone age man.'

Robert does a brilliant stone age man impression, with a blank unintelligent countenance and hands dangling long to his sides.

(Laughter)

'There he is, living in his cave. Ugh! ugh! He picks up his club or spear and goes out looking for food. Unsurprisingly he's walking to the last place where he found food.'

(Laughter)

'And there's Rat taking in all of the information.'

Robert does his hand cranked cine camera impression.

(Laughter)

'The information is coming in through eyes, ears, nose, mouth, skin.'

Robert walks up and down cranking away as if he is filming us.

'All of a sudden he hears this big clumping noise, boom boom boom. He feels the ground shake.'

Robert does an impression of someone trying to keep their balance as if the ground is shaking.

(Laughter)

'Now, Rat has received this information and he starts going through the records to see if he recognises any of these sensations. The best way he knows how to survive is to go through the old files.'

Robert turns to the side and again does an impression of someone opening the draw of a filing cabinet and leafing through documents.

'Hmm! Thumping noise - no record, ground shaking - no record. All of this time, the sound and the vibrations are getting closer. Then he catches sight of it. It's a great big hairy thing with tusks and a swinging trunk-like nose. Rat checks the records again. Hmm!'

Robert does his filing cabinet impression.

'It's not Jeff,' he says.

(Laughter)

'Nope, I haven't seen one of these before.'

Robert makes a bemused expression.

'Before Rat can decide what to do, the mammoth, because that's what it is if you weren't sure, has swung his trunk and knocked the caveman into a big pile of mammoth shit.'

(Laughter)

'He sails right through the air and into the heap of dung. Rat is

184

shaken up but he's still taking everything in. Ouch! That hurts. Phew! That stinks. He's a bit dazed, sort of semi-conscious, but OK. Rat has recorded all of the sensations and information and filed away the details. The caveman shakes himself of and ambles back to his cave to lick his wounds.'

Robert pauses and takes a breath.

'The caveman, though, still needs some food so, a bit later, he ventures out again to see what he can find to eat. All of the time Rat is taking in the information, processing it, recording it and filing it as usual.'

Again Robert does his cine camera impression.

'Then he hears it. Boom boom boom. He feels the ground shake. He sees the beast and hears the swish of the trunk. Rat checks the files. Loud noise, ground shaking, sound of trunk swinging. Association – pain, nasty smell of mammoth shit. I'm off.'

Robert exaggerates an impression of someone running away.

(Laughter)

'So, we can see, in very basic terms, how the rational mind processes and stores the multi-sensory information and re-uses that information for future encounters and experiences.'

Robert pauses again.

'Now think about it,' he continues. 'Another caveman's rational mind, his Rat, might have recorded a completely different experience with a mammoth. His experience might not be one of pain and dung and semi-consciousness. The experience that his Rat records might be quite different, it might be completely benign.'

Robert looks at us, still scrutinizing us to see if there is anyone who is not keeping up with what he is saying.

'We're all happy about how our Rat, our rational mind, receives and correlates information and how it re-uses that information?'

185

Again, he pauses for a few seconds. The trainees nod their heads a few say, 'Yes'.

'OK. So, let's take a look at what happens with us. We're sophisticated modern twentieth century beings aren't we? Well most of us are.'

(Laughter)

'We'll start at the beginning. What happens with a new born infant? The process is the same as the caveman. A new born child is a clean slate. It may have certain instincts like, go for the teat but it really only knows comfort or discomfort, basic pleasure or pain. It has no experiences to determine these instincts. Everything is new. What sort of things might the new born child experience?'

'Being born,' says Marjory.

'Yes. Good. The first thing,' says Robert. 'Being born. There you are, all nice and cosy and warm with pleasant subdued lighting, plugged in to a food source, very agreeable. And then, all of a sudden, you're out, into the cold, unplugged from the food source. There's an unpleasant bright light and you're getting a smack on the arse.'

(Laughter)

'So, out you come and there's Rat, he springs into life and says, "What the fuck is this!" and makes a record of the experience and sticks it in a file.'

(Laughter)

'Now I know that there is some opinion that says the process of rationality starts in the womb. There are sensations and experiences passed and shared with the mother. The unborn child may be affected by a multitude of stimuli. These may be on a rational level or be purely experiential. The fact of it is that we are not exactly sure when the rational mind is engaged. But, just for the sake of the point I want to get

186

across, for arguments sake, let's say that the process begins at birth. OK?'

Robert waits. There are nods from the trainees. Someone says, 'OK'.

'But don't we have inherent instincts as well?' asks Pat. 'Like fear of snakes for example.'

'Yes,' says Robert. 'Once again, there may be inherent animal or, in the example you gave, mammal instincts. There may be a form of collective consciousness and shared past experiential instinct passed genetically. These would have an impact on the rational mind and be accommodated in the files by Rat in the same way as physically acquired experience. With me?' Robert asks Pat.

'Yes, yes fine,' Pat replies.

'So, as before, for the sake of argument, let's focus on the rational mind and say that the process starts at birth. What other experiences are there likely to be after being born?'

'Being fed,' says Tania.

'Or not being fed,' says Mac.

'Being picked up,' says Snick.

'Or being dropped on your head like you,' says Robert.

(Laughter)

'Getting nappy rash.'

'Being held.'

'Being cuddled.'

There follows further suggestions of an infant's early experiences.

'So poor old rat is immediately busy recording a myriad of multi-sensory experiences all of which need to be filed,' says Robert. 'He

187

is being bombarded with new information. In our species, when we are young, our parents, especially our mothers, live to ensure our survival. Don't forget that most humans regard the passing on and survival of their genetic offspring as being part of the survival of their being. We will see, later, what happens when the child develops ego and their Rat becomes totally responsible for their own survival.'

Robert walks over to the stool and glances at the notes that are resting on top of it.

'OK,' he says, 'let's go back a bit. We have already talked about the survival of the mind. We have seen how Rat files all of the sensory information it receives. Let us have a look at the nature of these files.'

Robert pauses and looks at us. He has a serious expression on his face.

'This is a really important part of understanding how we operate,' he says. 'I want you to concentrate and *get* what I am going to explain to you.'

The trainees shift in their seats. Some lean forward slightly. It feels like Robert is purposely building up to a climax.

'OK. So let us look at the nature of the files. How they are made and what they do.'

Robert pauses.

'The first type of file is the one that deals with the primary purpose of the rational mind, namely, survival. This type of file is concerned with experiences like the caveman's interlude with the mammoth. It involves a threat to survival, pain, and semi-consciousness or an altered state of consciousness like you can get when experiencing extreme pain. It also often includes an impact or sudden shock. This type of file is called a primary or number one experience. For example, our caveman receives an impact – threat to survival, a bump on his head

188

provides pain after he was knocked into the heap of dung, which caused semi-consciousness. Now, every time he sees a mammoth he's off. Rat's got the file out, sees the recorded data and hits the flight button. Someone give me an example of a number one experience that a child may have?'

'Falling over and banging your head,' suggests Tania.

'OK,' says Robert. 'Let's say a girl, little Louisa, is in the garden playing with her brother Jack and their dog Rover. She is carrying her favourite doll. Louisa and Jack are chasing around the garden and Rover the dog is running around with them as well. She trips over and bangs her head. Impact - threat to survival. She feels pain. She's in a semi-conscious state. A classic primary or number one experience. She starts to recover and is aware that Rover the dog is snuffling her face and hair and Jack, her brother, is standing over her blocking out the sun. He is saying to her, "are you alright." The mother comes out, picks her up, hands her back her favourite doll, carries her into the house, gives her a piece of chocolate and a cuddle and tells her that everything will be fine. A complete number one or primary experience. Anyone remember anything like that happening to them?'

'I fell out of a tree once,' says Brian. 'I didn't bang my head but I was winded and shaken and semi-conscious.'

'Falling out of a tree is certainly a threat to survival. You were semi-conscious from being winded. Any pain?'

'Oh yeh! Plenty of pain. My father came and got me and picked me up. He put me back on my feet and was laughing.'

'That sounds like a first class primary experience,' says Robert.

'It was a sunny day. I was running through our house trying to get out into the garden. I must have been three or four years old. I tripped and cracked my head on the door frame. I cut my head open and had to go to the doctors,' says Celia. 'I had blood on my blouse. I didn't get to go

189

out in the garden that day.'

'The sight of you own blood often triggers a threat to survival as well as a bang on the head. You had both. You were semi-conscious and in pain,' says Robert. 'Definitely a primary experience.'

'But when a child is very young aren't all experiences going to be primary experiences?' asks Miranda.

'No, but many will be. If they involve a threat to survival, pain and altered consciousness they are primary experiences. What is the first primary experience we have? An experience where we are dragged from a really comfortable, warm and safe place with muted lights and muffled sounds into a cold, bright, inhospitable environment that definitely feels like a threat to our survival and involves pain and semi-consciousness. Come on. We alluded to it earlier.'

'Birth,' says someone.

'Yes, we all start our lives with a full on, grade A, primary experience. The first perceived threat to survival, a state of semi-consciousness and pain. Has everyone got what a number one or primary experience is?'

Robert pause for a few seconds.

'OK. Now we are going to look at another type of experience, the number two or secondary experience.'

Once again, a few people shift about in their seats. This is a long session. Everyone is alert and energised. There is a sense of anticipation that we are close to *getting it*. I am attempting to stay focused and hold what is being said in my mind.

'The secondary or number two experience is one where the mind experiences a sudden and traumatic loss accompanied by a strong, usually negative, emotion. There is, however, no threat to survival. The most obvious example is a sudden death, perhaps of a member of the child's family. However, if the sudden loss is of something other than death and is associated with a primary experience, it might not seem obvious or important, to another person but will seem to be of great importance to the person, the child, involved. Is everyone getting this?'

Heads nod. A few of the trainees say, 'Yes.'

'Let me give you an example. Our little girl Louisa finds Rover the dog dead in the kitchen.'

A few people go, 'Ahh!' in sympathy.

'Rover is old and he's had a good life.'

Robert looks to the ceiling as he re-assures us.

'It is a sudden and unexpected loss. However, there is no threat to survival. It is not a primary experience. But Rover is dead and Rover is associated with a primary experience. Remember, when she came round from falling over and hitting her head Rover was there, snuffling her face. So Little Louisa cries out. She goes over to Rover and strokes him. He is still and lifeless. Her mother comes in and sees poor old Rover dead on the floor. She picks up Louisa, carries her out of the kitchen gives her some chocolate and puts her on her bed. Louisa cries for a while and falls asleep. A secondary or number two experience.'

'But does the sudden loss have to be associated with the death of a loved one or a pet?' asks Jerry.

'No,' says Robert. 'Not necessarily. Remember, I said that the loss could relate to something else that was a part of a primary experience, something that may seem trivial to another person. Let's say that little Louisa loses her doll. She is on the train with her mother and brother and Rover the dog and she leaves it on the train and it's gone. When she realizes the doll is gone she starts to cry and her brother says,

191

"Are you alright." He then holds Rover up and Rover snuffles her face and sniffs around her hair. The doll was part of the primary experience. She was carrying it when she was chasing about with her brother and Rover. It was there when she fell. Her mother came and comforted her and handed her back the doll. The doll was an important part of the primary experience. In this secondary experience there is no threat to survival but her brother asked if she was alright and Rover snuffled and sniffed around her face and hair thus re-enforcing the connection. The loss of the doll may seem a trivial loss to someone else but for little Louisa, at that time, it is a sudden and traumatic loss. Yes Marjory.'

'In both experiences Louisa is given some chocolate. Would she, later in life, associate comfort with chocolate? Is that a number two experience?'

'No, that would be a number three experience. A number three experience is one that is associated with any primary or secondary experience. All number three experiences relate back to primary or secondary experiences. I'll give you an example. Let's go back to our cavemen and their mammoth experiences. We saw that the experience of the first caveman produced fear. Now let's say the other caveman we mentioned, who had a different experience with a mammoth, figures out that the beast is in fact, slow moving and relatively benign. He works out that if you manoeuvre yourself properly you can drop a boulder on the mammoth's head and get yourself a big supply of meat, some handy tusks and a nice mammoth rug. Now let us imagine that this caveman gives the rug to our first caveman, who has *the fear of mammoth primary experience*. He is going to wonder why he can never get a good night's sleep on the mammoth rug. It's a number three experience that relates back to the primary. It's like number three experiences that go back to being born. No wonder some people don't like hospitals.'

192

(Laughter)

'As Marjory mentioned. Remember little Louisa's primary experience. She bangs her head, she trips over, there's a threat to survival, she's in pain, she's semi-conscious. Her mum picks her up, comforts her and gives her some chocolate. OK! Here's a number three experience. Later in life, when Louisa feels she needs some comfort, what's she going to reach for? Especially if there's no one around to give her a cuddle.'

'Chocolate,' says Marjory enthusiastically.

(Laughter)

'But if this is the case, don't we carry these number three experiences through all of our lives, right through to adulthood?' asks Kenny.

'Yes of course,' says Robert. 'Imagine little Louisa is grown up and she's going out with a nice young man. Let's call him Harry. Now these two lovebirds have spent a nice afternoon at the coffee shop in town and they're walking back to Louisa's house through the park. They stop for a few minutes and sit on a bench. Harry leans over and gives Louisa a kiss. He grips her arm and, in his moment of passion, squeezes a little too hard. Louisa says, "Ow! That hurts," and Harry asks, "Are you alright?" At that moment, when she looks up, Harry is blocking out the sun. Louisa suddenly feels unwell. She wants to go home and have some chocolate and lie down. She has just had a classic number three experience.'

'But is Louisa associating all of this to her number one experience?' asks Kenny.

'Yes. This is how the mind works. Each element of the experience is linked. The association of the pain and the sun being blocked out and a male asking her if she is alright. In this instance her association leads to her wanting chocolate and a lie down.'

(Some laughter)

193

'In another similar situation she may end up marrying Harry because she loves it when he holds his face against hers and smells her hair. Like Rover the dog. She's not marrying Harry of course. She's marrying Rover the dog.'

(Laughter. Mostly by the males)

'I don't know what you're all laughing about,' says Robert. 'You will all probably end up marrying your mothers. I guarantee you that your mother is in at least one of your primary experiences apart from your first one of being born.'

(Laughter)

'And you ladies,' he continues. 'If you don't end up marrying your dog it is quite likely that it will be your father. Similarly, he is likely to be in at least one of your primary experiences.'

Robert pauses for a few seconds.

'This is a reasonably simplified explanation,' says Robert. 'The process by which multi sensory experiences are inter-related and associated with previous experiences is extremely complex. The crux of the matter is that Rat, your rational mind, is there taking everything in, recording and filing every new experience. These files are: number one or primary experiences, number two or secondary experiences and number three or tertiary experiences.'

'So you are saying that if, for example, I walk into a hospital, I might have a sense of uneasiness because something has stimulated a response that goes back to my primary experience of birth?' asks Jed.

'Yes, it could be the smell of the hospital, seeing a man in a white coat, the sound of rubber shoes squeaking on the floor or all of them. Like the smell of the mammoth rug.'

'OK, I get it,' says Jed.

'So, let's go back to the young child. From the moment the child is born it is bombarded with multi-sensory information. This information is arranged into files. The child's experience of being born is a number one experience. How many primary experiences might a child have in their first few years?'

'There must be hundreds of perceived threats to their survival. Children are always falling over and bumping into things, scrapping their knees and so on,' says Sandy.

'It depends on the child,' says Snick. 'If a child is more adventurous he'll get into more scrapes.'

Robert nods his head in a non-committal way.

'There must be loads of experiences with all of the factors that make up a number one experience,' says Celia.

'What if a child is falling asleep and a toy falls over on his head? There is an impact – a threat to survival. The child feels pain, it's semi-conscious 'cos of the sleep,' says Sarah. 'That would be a primary experience wouldn't it?'

'Yes,' says Robert. 'A number one experience and the kid didn't even have to get out of bed.'

(Laughter)

'And remember, that in its first year, a child spends much of the time in a semi-conscious state,' Robert adds.

'So if a child is simply carried from a warm house to outside where it's freezing cold; if the child is in a semi-conscious state its Rat might see the sensation of the cold as pain and a threat to survival,' says James.

Robert nods his head.

'Well given how many times a child is handled and bumped around, there must be hundreds,' says Mac.

'And how many secondary experiences related to those primary experiences do you think there would be?' asks Robert.

'Depends who dies,' says Ray.

(Some laughter)

'Not necessarily,' says Robert. 'Remember little Louisa's doll is lost. The doll is associated with survival. She was handed back the doll during her number one experience. It might seem an insignificant loss to us but not to Louisa because of the association.'

'What about number three experiences and all of the other stimuli a child receives?' asks Jules. 'There must be hundreds of thousands.'

'They're all being perceived, recorded and catalogued by Rat.'

Robert does his hand cranked cine camera impression.

(Laughter)

'You are right Jules. There will be a huge quantity of number three experiences. Again, like the caveman's mammoth rug. And, as you say, don't forget the associated number three files that are made. The sight of Grandpa's hands might be associated with the doctor's hands at the time of birth or Aunty Flo's smell might be like the midwife's. The call of a bird might be associated with being taken outside into the cold.'

'But there must be more than hundreds of thousands of stimuli and associations,' says Dan. 'There must be millions. Aren't they all associated back to secondary and primary experiences?'

'Yes and as I mentioned before these are also inter-related and associated so the grey of the hospital blanket gets associated with grey sky, grey pavements, grey walls. The hospital floor gets associated with all floors, the midwife's hands get associated with women's hands which gets associated with hands in general and then people. Having your hair smelt might relate to a past number one or number two experience so that hair carries its own associations. And these associations are just the ones related to the early primary experiences. Never mind the rest of the primary experiences.'

Robert pauses for a few seconds.

'So how many files do you think get made in the first few years of a child's life?' he asks.

'The process must give rise to exponential growth,' says Mac. 'The numbers of files must be enormous, vast.'

'And the brain's ability to store information is finite. Although everyone has a different capability, there is only so much storage space available in the filing cabinets,' says Robert.

Robert is standing in the middle of the room, in front of the stool.

'So, here is the question. How many of the child's vast quantity of files are related to the automatic survival response?'

'All of them,' says Dan.

Again Robert pauses.

'All of them,' he replies. 'By the time the child is around four or five years old it is full up. There is no more room in the filing cabinets. Every emotion that you experience after that age is associated back to what happened before you were five years old. Everything you get, right now, as adults, is stimulus – response, stimulus – response triggered by a perceived threat to your survival before you were five.'

The room has gone quiet. What Robert is saying is gradually sinking in to the trainees. For me it is like a clearing mist as the meaning becomes apparent.

'Every emotion?' asks Cally. 'But what about if I get angry when I've just missed the bus or something like that?'

'Your anger is a response that goes back to a primary experience that happened before you were five.'

'Even if I can't remember it?'

'Even if you can't remember it,' Robert replies. 'That's why some people don't like certain things and others aren't bothered. That's why Simon gets anger when he hears swearwords and other people just laugh. That's why some people fear the dentist and others don't. Different stimuli, different survival threats, different primary experiences. All auto-responses that go back to perceived threats to survival that occurred before you were five.'

Again Robert waits. He is watching us. Watching, as what he has been saying is grasped by the trainees. A number of trainees are sitting with their mouths open. Others have serious expressions on their faces.

'The fact of the matter is: you are all robots,' he says. 'Mechanically playing back the responses in your files. All of your emotions just triggered by some past threat to survival. It's been staring you in the face all of your lives. You're robots.'

Robert shrugs his shoulders.

'You are all robots.'

Some of the trainees have now started to laugh. Some still sit with open mouths, some look bewildered. Simon looks livid.

'Do you *get it*?' Robert asks. 'That is all there is to *get*. Do you *get* that you are robots?'

I turn to James, who is seated next to me. His eyes widen and he starts to laugh. More trainees are laughing now.

'That's it. You are robots. You were robots before the seminar and you're robots now. Two hundred quid and you're just the same. You're still robots.'

More and more people are smiling and laughing now.

'You've spent your whole lives pretending that you had some

sort of control over how you feel, some determination about who you are or how you behave. Pointless, you're robots.'

'I thought we were supposed to get enlightened,' Simon spurts out his words angrily.

'Enlightenment is knowing you're a robot,' says Robert.

(Huge laughter)

'How do you feel Simon?' asks Robert.

'I'm angry.'

'Of course you are,' says Robert. 'You are a robot. Be angry, don't try and change it. Take what you get.'

(More laughter)

'Well I feel great,' says Jed laughing.

'Jed, you get joy. You're a robot. Don't try and change it. Take what you get.'

(Laughter)

'I find it a bit depressing. I mean, to find out I'm a robot,' says Celia.

This makes some people laugh even louder.

'I can't see why everyone is laughing,' she says.

The laughter goes up another notch.

'I mean, if we are machines what should we do?'

'Get oiled,' offers Snick.

(More laughter)

'Have I got it?' continues Celia.

She gives a pleading look to Robert.

'Some people are getting joy and you are getting grief Celia. You are a robot. Take what you get and don't try and change it.'

'Oh fuck it,' she says and sits.

There is laughter and applause for Celia. She starts to laugh and

199

stands again.

'I mean, fuck it!' she says laughing.

'You mean I've just sat here for two weekends, got a sore arse, been bored out of my mind, spent two hundred notes and that's it. I'm a robot?' says Brian.

'Yep!' says Robert. 'You are a robot. You're two hundred quid light and you've got a sore arse. You were a robot when you came in and you're a robot now.'

'Fucking brilliant,' says Brian.

(Laughter)

'What are you getting Brian?'

'Joy. Unmitigated fucking delight.'

'Take what you get Brian. You're a robot.'

'Is that all there is?' asks Kate.

'That's it,' says Robert. 'I know a few of you are sitting there thinking, that can't be right, he's going to spin it around in a moment and we'll be able to change ourselves and everything will be alright. Sorry. There is no more. You're all robots and the thought that whizzed through your mind saying, there has to be more is an automatic response to a stimulus that is associated back to a perceived threat to your survival before you were five. You Kate, are a robot.'

(Laughter)

'Are you a robot?' asks Jules.

'Yes, I am a robot.'

As Robert replies he frowns in an expression of solemnity and seriousness.

'We robots who know we are robots are enlightened,' he says in a deep, serious voice.

(Huge laughter)

200

'But surely, if you look at what Kant says.' It is Simon.

When he says the name Kant, Simon's words are drowned out by laughter and he sits down with a flop.

'You are robots,' Robert continues. 'All of your little upsets, all of your anger, all of your fear, all of your joy, all just your robot mind playing back some past threat to survival. You can't help it. You have no control over the experience or emotion you get. You are robots.'

The energy in the room has increased to a level not seen in the previous days of the seminar. There are continued pockets of laughter as people share their experience. I feel a massive surge of energy like I have been pushing against a door and it has just burst open.

'I'm happy to be a robot,' says Jaclyn.

She is laughing.

'You are a robot. You get joy. Take what you get. You are all robots and the only thing you can do is take what you get and don't try and change it.'

After twenty minutes or so of people sharing what they are getting Robert tells us that we're going to have a short break before we finish.

'There are some refreshments laid out in the room next door,' he says. 'We can't let you out onto the streets until you're a little more grounded. We've promised not to let one hundred and forty enlightened robots out onto the street until they've calmed down.'

There is more laughter and then loud applause for Robert - and ourselves.

201

There is water, squash, tea, coffee and some biscuits laid out on trestle tables in the adjoining room. I pour myself some water. Although everyone's energy levels remain high there is not so much chatter as I might have expected. If I had to sum up the mood and demeanour of the trainees I would say that they look satisfied.

After half an hour everyone has managed to get some refreshment and we return to our seats in the studio room next door.

Robert enters the room to long and enthusiastic applause. He spends the next half an hour or so giving us a magnificent demonstration of his skills of impression. Not only does he imitate people's voices perfectly but he also mimics their mannerisms. It is a truly masterful performance that makes me laugh so much that my face hurts.

'And there's Snick saying, "I fancy Kim, like, you know. I hoped this wouldn't get read out but I'm glad it did 'cos I'd never have the courage to say it to her face otherwise, would I?" Now he'll be able to woo her with a presentation of his prize leeks.'

(Laughter)

'And Arthur, "I can't wait to get out of this room. There's a pie with my name on it out there." I could hear his stomach rumbling from the front of the room.'

(Laughter)

'And Carol, she couldn't speak in public without shaking, "I'm so timid but I'm becoming less so now I've realised that my timidity is a racket." Now we can't shut her up.'

(Laughter)

'OK! OK!' says Robert.

He waits until the laughter at his final impression subsides.

'I'm going to clear up a few things before we let you out,' he says. 'Remember, we still create the world around us and we still need to assume responsibility for it even if, as robots, we can't choose what emotion we get around it. When it comes to our experience we have to take what we get. If we give up wanting and trying to change what we get, then, there can be a transformation. Remember, persistence causes change.'

Robert sits on the stool. It is the first time that I have seen him sit down.

'There is an area of choice that I want to cover,' he continues. 'We know that we can't prove that we weren't created five minutes ago with all of our memories and experiences intact. So we cannot say with total certainty that the past is real. We also know that there is no way of knowing when we'll die. There is nothing to say that we will live another ten minutes. Everything that we do could be the last thing that we do. All we can really rely on is our experience in the here and now, the present. So we don't have any choice over our past, we don't have any choice over our experience in the present, owing to the fact that we are robots.'

(Some laughter)

'And we have no choice over when we're going to die. I'll give you an example. A man is walking through a ravine and he stops to tie up his shoelace and a boulder drops a few metres in front of where he's stopped, where he would have been if he hadn't stopped to tie his lace. If he had continued walking - kaput! He would be dead, crushed by the boulder. Conversely he could have stopped to tie his lace a few meters further on and the boulder could have dropped on him because he

203

stopped. He has no choice over when he dies. He has only one choice.'

Robert pauses for a few seconds.

'And that is how he ties his shoelace. He either chooses to tie it the best he can, tie it beautifully, with care, or not. That is his only choice: whether to tie his shoelace impeccably or not.'

Again Robert pauses for a few seconds.

'Can anyone tell me, what is the main component of acting impeccably? We covered this during the first weekend.'

'Giving one hundred percent,' says Brian.

'OK, but how do we give one hundred percent.'

'When we have nothing going on,' says Celia.

'Exactly,' says Robert. 'When we have nothing going on. When we are acting with our beliefs suspended, acting without our beliefs, with nothing going on. That is when we can give one hundred percent that is when we can act impeccably. That is when we can tie our shoelace beautifully.'

Robert moves from the stool where he has been sitting.

'Do you remember, last week, I added two more base experiences?'

'Satisfaction and responsibility,' says Marjory.

'Yes. Satisfaction comes from joy. I think you all got that when you realized that you are robots.'

We laugh and nod our heads in agreement. Someone, Jed I think, says, 'YES,' really loudly.

'Responsibility, the experience above satisfaction, comes from knowing that you are a robot, knowing that you create the world, knowing that you have to assume responsibility for being in the world and knowing that, in a world of choices, your only real choice is the way in which you tie your shoelace in the ravine.'

Robert then gets us to sit quietly with our eyes closed for a few moments.

'Take a few breaths and relax,' he says. 'You are graduates now and there are a few people who would like to acknowledge you for *getting it*.'

I hear the doors to the studio room open.

'OK, open your eyes,' says Robert.

I open my eyes and look up. Incredibly, a crowd of fifty or sixty people come in like a tidal wave. They are applauding us. The crowd is made up of the people who had recommended us to the seminar along with the trainers and a number of other graduates from previous seminars. When they have all poured into the room they stand and acknowledge us with their applause which rises to a crescendo. For all of us trainees, now graduates, it is an intensely joyous and moving moment.

Final Wednesday evening

The final Wednesday session is held at the Metropole hotel on the Edgware Road. Probably because Programmes is in full working operation on weekdays.

Robert enters the room to tumultuous applause. I turn to watch him walking along the side of the seats to the front. As I turn I see Kim, standing at the back of the room.

This session is mostly taken up with reminders about giving up wanting to change our experience and taking responsibility. It is a laughter filled occasion with the usual mimicking of the graduates' traits. Robert and Kim are consummate performers. As I mentioned before, Robert, especially, has a tremendous talent for impressions. Once again his impersonations of the graduates are hilarious. We graduates are still completely high on the experience of having *got it*. The experience of succeeding in completing the seminar in an environment of mutual support has created a bond between the graduates. It is a bond of shared knowledge and experience. Our enthusiasm and feeling of mutual satisfaction is tangible. It is a feeling come alive, like Prospero's tempest. A number of the graduates are eager to share some of the changes that have occurred in their lives in the last couple of days.

'I want to share that, when I got home on Sunday evening, my psychologist friend was waiting for me,' says Caroline.

Caroline takes a deep breath.

'Well, when I got in he asked me how it had gone and I said that it was great. And with that I ripped his clothes off and we had sex on the floor in the living room.'

(Laughter)

'It was wonderful.'

(More laughter and applause)

Caroline is beaming cheekily from ear to ear.

'When I came here I had a bit of a superiority complex.'

It is Simon.

(Laughter)

Today he is wearing blue denim jeans, an open necked shirt and a new looking cotton jacket. I wonder if he has dumped the elbow patch look for good.

'I want to share that I still have it. I still feel superior to everyone else but now I don't give a fuck.'

(Laughter)

'I also wanted to swear to point out that it is not an issue any more.'

(Applause and laughter)

'I want to share that I have dumped my husband,' says Cally, the Canadian lady. 'When I told him he was almost not surprised. He has agreed to do the next seminar though. So you never know.'

Cally is smiling as she sits.

(Applause)

'I want to share that my ex husband and I have decided to try again in our relationship,' says Cath. 'He did the seminar and then got me to do it so we are a lot less rackety.'

(Laughter)

'We are going to see if we can allow each other to exist in our space.'

(Applause)

It is interesting how we spontaneously return to acknowledging people's sharing with applause. It is strange but it seems OK now, almost the natural thing to do.

It is also good to hear how completing the seminar has had an impact on peoples' lives. I imagine that this is one of the reasons why this last Wednesday session is held. It is also interesting to note that all of the graduates, without exception, appear energised, purposeful and confident. I believe that this is not just because of being in the safe and comfortable environment of fellow graduates. These new found traits extend beyond the seminar environment and out into the world, the graduates' individual worlds.

Another reason why we are here, of course, is to introduce new prospective trainees to the seminar. We have been asked to bring two people along to the preview that is being held in another room and many people, me included, do in fact bring at least one person. I suppose that this in itself is not a bad thing. It is, after all, the most efficient and effective way of recruiting people for the seminar. Also, I genuinely believe that the seminar will prove beneficial to the person I have introduced.

In addition to introducing new prospective trainees we are offered the chance to undertake further courses such as the Financial Independence and Abundance course. Probably fifteen percent of the graduates sign up for this programme.

We are also given the opportunity to work for Programmes Ltd. either in a full or part time capacity. In reality less than five percent of all graduates involve themselves with Programmes Ltd.

When I leave the hotel I say goodbye to my fellow graduates. Some I keep in contact with. Some I won't see again until thirty one years later when I write this book.

Part 3

A Different Viewpoint

After the Seminar

After I had completed the seminar I was often asked about the people who I did the seminar with: the other trainees.

'What were they like before the seminar?'

'They were pretty much like any group of people,' I said. 'I got on well with a few of them, some of the others were nice people, some less nice and one or two were complete idiots.'

'What about after the seminar.'

'They became enlightened.'

'What about the ones who were idiots?'

'They became enlightened idiots.'

Where did it come from and where did it go?

Exegesis was formulated by Robert D'Aubigny. It was taken, almost completely, from Erhard Seminar Training or EST. The basis of EST itself was drawn from a number of different sources including, Gestalt therapy, Psycho-analysis, Zen Buddhism, the Tao, Shamanism and Scientology.

The EST training took place over four days. Participants were taken through various processes that allowed them to become enlightened or, in their words, to *get it*, that is, to finally understand how our minds work, how we operate as beings and to be aware of the truth about how our lives actually are.

Robert D'Aubigny, very cleverly, took Werner Erhard's EST and remodelled it from the US orientated programme to a more UK friendly one. The structure of EST fitted the American psyche brilliantly and Exegesis resonated with the British in the same way.

At five whole days and three evenings the Exegesis seminar programme was longer than the EST programme. But whilst Exegesis was extremely demanding and taxing, it was less *in your face* than EST. You could say that, compared to EST, Exegesis was almost polite. This politeness was, in the main, engendered by the attitudes and behaviour of the Exegesis trainees who, in my observation, wished to avoid confrontation more than their American counterparts. The Exegesis

213

trainees tended to be more receptive to the notion of participation in the development of the themes that ran through the programme. Additionally the British trainees seemed less concerned with being mocked or joked about. They were more willing to laugh at themselves. All of these traits were parts of the British nature, ones that Robert D'Aubigny recognised and accounted for.

What Robert did, and what was part of his genius, was to inject more humour and joy into the process whilst not diminishing the effect. Another part was his knowing that this would resonate with a British audience that was perhaps more self effacing than an American one.

He was not alone in understanding that the path to enlightenment needs to touch the soul, and that this is best done through laughter.

After both seminar programmes a connection or bond is formed between those who completed the respective programmes. In EST the connection was of a jointly experienced journey and shared secret. With Exegesis, whilst there was the same feeling of membership and knowledge held in common, there was, throughout the seminar, more emphasis on mutual support between the trainees. It was almost as if there was a collective desire for everyone in the group to successfully complete the programme. Additionally, whilst EST was inherently theatrical in the nature of its presentation, Exegesis carried this theatricality further by making greater use of theatrical role playing. In fact, the scene in the seminar room, at times, resembled a soap opera.

There were further differences between the two programmes on an operational level. The Exegesis programme was more practically orientated than EST with a greater emphasis placed on using the psychological and physical benefits of completing the seminar in day to day life. Exegesis focused more on the transformation of experience, especially in terms of dealing with what was known as unwanted, continued, persistent experiences.

Another departure from the EST format was the issue of personal responsibility. With Exegesis this was more focused on the nature of choice rather than, as with EST, the concept that we create our experience and therefore the world. Exegesis promoted the notion that the trainee should choose to assume responsibility for being in the world and demonstrated the tangible benefits that could be obtained from that viewpoint.

As I mentioned before, Exegesis was more performance orientated than EST. Although there was a great sense of theatricality with EST I recognised that Exegesis used a number of theatre therapy techniques. Perhaps this was because Robert D'Aubigny had been an actor and consequently may well have been familiar with these types of practices.

The fact that Robert was a consummate performer with an exquisite sense of comedy timing and an enormous talent for doing impressions of people meant that his personality often dominated the training. Similarly Kim possessed a strong personality and in many ways was as charismatic as Robert.

I am sure that some of the negativity surrounding Exegesis came about due to the strength of the personalities of Robert and Kim. Whilst being inherently true that Robert was the leader of Exegesis, the fact that it appeared to be so encouraged further spurious claims of a personality cult.

It had been a similar situation with EST and Werner Erhard. Werner Erhard's advantage was that he took a step back from the limelight of actually presenting his seminars. Although partly done to accommodate the possibility of greater numbers of people participating in the EST programme, Erhard trained other people to undertake the roles of main trainers. This action had the effect of removing or diluting the notion of a personality cult type scenario.

There was a further misunderstanding of D'Aubigny's motives due to the fact that he knew there to be a massive potential benefit in harnessing the tremendous energy and creativity that exploded from people who completed the seminar. D'Aubigny constantly sought ways to exploit this and it meant that, to some people, there would always be a question mark over his motives. It was this, along with the headline seeking media attention that I believe, finally became too much of a battle and Exegesis stopped operating as a seminar programme.

After the Exegesis seminar programme ceased to operate, Programmes Ltd and later The Merchants Group, as it became, went on to enjoy considerable commercial success.

It is difficult to find too many negatives about the Exegesis seminar. If I had to pick out some adverse aspects of the programme I would say that at five days and three evenings it was a day too long. I suspect that the additional time was allowed to accommodate concepts that would be useful to the trainee should they have decided to join Programmes Ltd. Additionally, whilst not being aggressive, there was a bit of a sell to get involved and join Programmes Ltd. Once again though, I must point out that it was a matter of choice whether to do so. It is an often overlooked fact that proportionately, very few graduates chose to involve themselves with Exegesis or Programmes.

How It Works

As far as I know there has been no valid scientific research carried out to determine the effectiveness of the Exegesis seminar. It is difficult therefore, to provide any evaluation other than a subjective one.

There were, however, two studies carried out on EST that I am aware of. The most comprehensive of these was a study on the effectiveness of the EST programme completed in the nineteen seventies by Robert Ornstein and Associates that showed there to be a tangible and lasting effect which over ninety nine percent of the graduates deemed to be a positive one. Additionally, the study found no examples of anybody being harmed by attending the programme. Given the similarities between the two programmes, some conclusions may be drawn from that.

After completing the seminar in nineteen eighty three, I talked with almost one hundred graduates and the vast majority reported a positive outcome and regarded the seminar as a life changing experience. Thirty years later I again talked with a number of graduates and, as before, the vast majority said they had remained deeply affected, in a positive way, by the experience. Interestingly, most observed that the ideas first used on the seminar had entered the mainstream and formed the basis of many modern training methods, from self help to sales training. Additionally, many were also amused that some of the expressions first heard on the seminar had become commonplace.

My summary then, and again I must point out that it is a subjective one, is that the seminar worked. People *got it*. The seminar changed their lives in a positive way and it remained valid for the graduates throughout their lives.

So how does the seminar work?

The seminar works by placing the participants in a position where they are made to experience a variety of emotions. At the time, the trainees are unaware that they are, in effect, being tricked into experiencing these emotions. The long sessions in the room without access to food, water, lavatory and nicotine, the non approval of the trainers, the provoked confrontations, the sharing of the trainees' personal experiences and the various processes are designed to induce what are referred to as the basic emotions of apathy, grief, fear, anger, pride and joy.

Another of the vehicles used is the setting of agreements. The repetition and routine of the strict structure of when and how to communicate (sharing), the acknowledgment of those who have shared and not being able to sit next to someone you know or have sat next to before, stimulates further these emotional experiences in the trainees. By forbidding the use of alcohol, recreational drugs and non prescription pain relief drugs for the duration of the seminar it is virtually assured that the trainees will confront their experience rather than avoiding it in their day to day lives. With the restriction of no smoking whilst in the room, those trainees who smoke are in fact subjected to a much higher level of non avoidance of experience during the sessions due to nicotine withdrawal. The removal of personal items when entering the room, once again, stimulates an experience which the trainees slowly come to

218

identify and confront, similarly with the restriction on watches and the covering of the clocks.

The enlightenment notebooks and pencils and the strict adherence to time keeping and the agreements in general are designed to allow for a physical illustration of certain aspects of personal responsibility.

These methods provide a non intellectual description of experience and responsibility that transmits these concepts to the trainees' bodies. This is in much the same way as learning a musical instrument and acquiring 'finger memory'. For example, you could have explained to you, on an intellectual level, everything required to play the piano. However, until your body has learnt (in this instance hands fingers and feet) it would not be possible to play. Hence the assertion that one could sleep through the entire seminar and still *get it* at the end.

Having been stimulated into the above mentioned basic emotions, the trainees are then directed to identify exactly what emotion it is that they are experiencing at any given time. Having identified the emotion the trainees are instructed to *confront* their experience rather than avoid it. They are shown how to get it touch with it and how to experience it fully. They are provided with pointers such as: What is the physical sensation? Where in the body is it? What colour is it? Is it heavy or light? Whilst acknowledging and exploring their experience the trainees are told to give up trying to change it. Giving up trying to change the emotion has the effect of *disappearing* it or transforming it into a more positive one.

At the same time the participants are encouraged to take responsibility for creating their emotion and in fact for everything that

219

occurs in their world.

The idea of assuming complete personal responsibility for everything that we encounter is an extremely powerful and liberating practice. We encounter the world by intercepting information perceived through our senses and filtering that information through our acquired beliefs to create an emotion. By taking responsibility not only for this process but also for our acquired beliefs a new world of choice is opened up. Decisions become more considered and effective. One becomes aware of possibilities and accounts for them. For example: even if you get run over whilst crossing the road you have to take responsibility for choosing to cross the road, for choosing to put yourself in a situation where getting run over is a possibility. (Of course, as Robert pointed out, don't tell that to the insurance company. You have to take responsibility for them not wanting to pay you out.)

After a very short time of assuming responsibility, decision making skills become heightened and a previously undiscovered level of effectiveness as well as clarity of intent and purpose are developed.

All of the above procedures are structured to take the trainee through various conceptual stages. The format involves the progression of ideas presented intellectually and physically that lead to the trainees becoming aware, in a climax, that their emotional responses are automatic and stimulated by perceived threats to survival that happened in their lives before they were four or five years of age. In the climax in which the participants *get it* there is a tremendous feeling of release and joy at the realization that we have no choice over the emotion we create. As I have noted previously the outpouring of energy and creativity that accompanies this understanding is quite spectacular. Put simply, it is as if a weight has been shed. There is a profound sense of satisfaction and a lightness of being that is tangible.

As I have mentioned before, much of the seminar was steeped in a sense of theatre. This included the dramatic endings to the seminars of which there were a variety. All were moving and memorable. Their theatricality somehow re-enforcing the strength of the seminar experience.

Finally, I feel I have to emphasise the fact that although this book demonstrates the principals and working elements of the seminar and even provides a sensation of the elation and release involved in *getting it*, I must point out that the intensity of emotion and the physical experience of participating and completing the seminar can never be re-created in a book.

Printed in Great Britain
by Amazon.co.uk, Ltd.,
Marston Gate.